THINNING FROM THE INSIDE OUT

THINNING FROM THE INSIDE OUT

The Proven, Personal Approach to
Permanent Weight Loss

Elizabeth Lay

BANTAM BOOKS

TORONTO • NEW YORK • LONDON • SYDNEY • AUCKLAND

This book is dedicated to Linda R. Cunningham and
Melinda W. Mettler, the two most significant
women in my life

THINNING FROM THE INSIDE OUT
A Bantam Book / March 1986

Library of Congress Cataloging-in-Publication Data

Lay, Elizabeth.
  Thinning from the inside out.

  Bibliography: p. 189
  1. Reducing diets.   2. Reducing—Psychological aspects.
I. Title.
RM222.2.L377   1986   613.2'5   84-91001
ISBN 0-553-05076-1

Published simultaneously in the United States and Canada

PRINTED IN THE UNITED STATES OF AMERICA

BP   0 9 8 7 6 5 4 3 2 1

Contents

Acknowledgments

FROM MY HEART, I THANK the following individuals for their council, their support, and especially their contributions, often unknowingly made, to my understanding and assimilation of key ingredients for living thin, and then writing about it all.

To my parents, *in memoriam:* Your legacies of self-reliance and self-honesty proved more deeply ingrained in me than the unhealthy food relationship I developed, mostly when you weren't looking.

To my brothers, Britt and Rick: Your steadfast love and respect taught me something essential about permanence: the really important things in life are.

To Roger H. L. Wilson, M.D.: "Don't just try it, do it." You gave me back my life, Roger. God bless you. To Nancy L. Wilson, R.D.: You helped put nutrition and my relationship with food into a healthy perspective I could live thin on for the rest of my life.

To Mary C. Tall, Ph.D., clinical psychologist: We have known each other all our lives. Until we worked on this book together, I always thought of you as the master key maker. Then you taught me how to make my own. Finally, you showed me how to teach others—with compassion, patience, and especially honesty.

To Shelley Singer, Katherine Cross Worthington, and Joyce Cole: If friends be the sustenance of self-confidence, I believe.

To Leslie Cooper: You taught me what the sound of laughter really is. It is lighter than a pound of body fat, and also warmer.

To Gareth Esersky: Your personal tenacity reminded me of my own, and I took both to the swimming pool for a healthy workout.

To Jeannine Hager: Your persuasive powers are exceeded only by your patience and belief in what is right. The menus in this book are for you.

To Margaret T. Barker: It was in the Connecticut house that I discovered the keys to living thin emotionally. To Ann Macfarlane: You helped me see the difference between simply having a choice and actively making one.

To Bobbie Bristol, Charlotte Mayerson, Sandi Mendelson, Sydny Miner, Ann Patty, and Faith Sale: Never having been thin before, I looked for role models in women whose fashionable appearance, balanced attitudes, and confident feelings about themselves exuded a personal style I wanted to emulate. All of you unknowingly served as my principal role models.

To Constance Leisure, former book editor for *Ladies' Home Journal:* You started me writing about it all, Connie. To Joyce Engleson: You told me to write my own diet book, and I did. To Hope Dellon: You asked some of the toughest and most searching questions about the complexities of being overweight, and you wanted truthful answers.

To Larry Ashmead: I didn't forget the men. To Brad Miner: You're a better role model than Robert Redford. Even more, your astute perceptions about this program sent me in directions I didn't know I had the courage to go.

To Harvey Ginsberg and Bill Whitehead: Your personal delight in knowing I was writing this book gave me much-needed encouragement to sit down and do it.

To Manuela Soares, writing pal: I discovered on my own the love of reading. You helped me discover the love of writing.

To Dennison Demac, book confidant extraordinaire: You

showed me how to do it, Denny, to turn a blank piece of paper into a real manuscript page.

Finally, to Carol Mann, my literary agent, friend, and colleague: My gratitude is truly inexpressible for all that you have done for me. I am a better person for knowing you.

Introduction

WHEN ASKED BY MY PATIENT, Elizabeth Lay, to write an intro-
duction to her book, I was excited by the possibility. One does
not have to be a medical physician (as I am) to have witnessed,
in the last ten years, and especially in the last year, the re-
emphasis on diet and nutrition in our society. Concurrently,
there is a resurgence of information in the medical literature on
the importance of diet and weight loss in preventing health
problems as well. For years I have been in private practice with
a specialty in arthritis and have seen, firsthand, the magnitude
of problems that can be caused by being overweight. Although
I do not have special training in the treatment of obesity, I have
long been seeking a fully integrated approach to help my patients control their weight.

In July 1985, a leading medical journal, *Annuals of Internal Medicine*, published an article titled "Health Implications
of Obesity: A National Institute's of Health Consensus Develop-
ment Conference Statement." This report emphasized once
again that obesity, or increased fat storage, has adverse effects
on health and longevity. Being overweight is clearly associated
with high blood pressure, increased fats in the blood, sugar
diabetes, certain cancers, and other medical problems.

On the contrary, the role of exercise and its resulting

health benefits has been increasingly emphasized in the last ten years. As an avid runner and calorie-watcher, I know first-hand that exercise and a proper diet are important elements of weight-loss success.

Elizabeth Lay's personal approach to permanent weight loss certainly agrees with the present medical information on diet and exercise. With striking insight and honesty, she adds her own personal touch to the current body of knowledge. Elizabeth admits that permanent weight loss is difficult, but she points out through her own experience that a multistage approach to the problem can work. As I read the book I was impressed by her insights into the problem, which showed both an understanding of the psychological introspection needed to approach the task and maintain weight loss, and the nutritional requirements for a good, medically approved diet. Elizabeth does not promise immediate success but emphasizes that one must first gain a "thinning perspective." In layman's terms, she describes behavioral modification techniques that are helpful in changing one's learned responses to food. In addition, she emphasizes cooperative group therapy which is one of the oldest and probably the most successful way to lose weight.

Coupled with these psychological techniques, Elizabeth describes a medically sound, low-calorie diet, which has been shown to be safe when done under close medical supervision. Of course, any specific diet should be cleared with a physician so that individual medical problems can be considered.

Beyond the actual diet, Elizabeth deals with maintenance techniques to help overcome one of the major stumbling blocks to any low-calorie diet—boredom. Finally, she addresses other psychological problems that may occur in dealing with the new physical changes that are taking place within the body.

The physical changes do promote increased energy, and as Elizabeth points out, it is at this point that most people begin exercising. This time delay between starting a diet and beginning an exercise program is necessary since simply suggesting to an overweight person to start swimming, walking, or jogging rarely proves successful. Elizabeth believes, as I do, that exercise is one of the keys to "living thin" emotionally.

Do I think this approach can work? To answer this, I cite my original encounter with the author. Elizabeth had developed an inflammatory condition that required the use of corticosteroids, a potent medication that invariably causes increased appetite, salt retention, and subsequent weight gain. By following her personal approach, Elizabeth did not gain weight, and in fact she was able to lose six pounds while on this medication! This is a rare feat, and one that I certainly would like to see achieved by my other patients.

THINNING FROM THE INSIDE OUT: Your Personal Guide to Permanent Weight Loss by Elizabeth Lay is a comprehensive guide to weight loss structured by an intelligent woman who has integrated her personal experience into a psychological, medically sound, and practical approach to permanent weight loss.

I learned from this book. I hope readers will too.

C. Michael Neuwelt, M.D.

Oakland, California, November 1985

PART ONE

Preparations for Thinning from the Inside Out

CHAPTER ONE

Defining the Program

I HAD BEEN FOLLOWING MY personal diet plan for almost twelve months when, one late-August morning in 1981, I took my coffee out to the front porch and sat in the sun. After fifteen minutes, I got up and rubbed my backside, sore from sitting on the wooden steps. I felt my bones, how close they were to the skin. I stood and stretched to my full height—five feet one inch— feeling my hip bones, my rib cage, my spine. With a sense of urgency and disbelief I ran inside, undressed, and stood before my full-length mirror. No hips, no ass, no flab.

I, Elizabeth Lay, literary agent, former teacher, business manager, clerk-typist, and one-time telephone operator, had been overweight all my life. I had never known how I would look at my ideal weight. Even while slimming down on my self-designed diet program, my eyes had not believed what they saw, until that moment.

I remember smiling to myself as I looked in the mirror. My whole body smiled back at me. I gazed intently at my reflection. My eyes traveled downward from my neck, which no longer had three chins, and across shoulders now broad and straight, not round and puffy, not bulging into arms that just twelve months earlier had been as full and fat as watermelons. I could now count my ribs with my eyes alone. My breasts now jutted out; before, three times larger, they had lain passively

3

against my abdomen—a Santa Claus belly without jolliness.

That day as I stood in front of the mirror, I put my hands on my hips and wrapped my fingers into the curves of the bones. I could touch my index fingers together as they stretched across my flat stomach, my thumbs still firmly anchored to the curves just above my hips. My waist looked tiny. I had never before even known I had one.

I smiled as I looked at my thighs and down my legs. Gone were the mountains of flesh and flab that once had looked like elephant stumps, thunder thighs that seemed to rumble the ground as I walked.

I could even see my feet now. They looked small, like the rest of me. I could see the tendons on the tops of my feet when I flexed my toes. I had never seen them before; layers of fat had buried them deep inside. They looked a little strange, though, stretched taut like a tightrope.

The backs of my hands and the outsides of my forearms were, I think, what I loved most during that moment of thin recognition. The big veins in my forearms were slightly elevated, and when I moved my wrists up and down, the muscles flexed. They seemed to dance, and I felt very strong. The veins on my hands, too, were raised. I could see them clearly, and feel them when I ran my fingertips over them. I felt incredibly alive.

I used to think I began my diet, weighing 240 pounds, because I had been scared into it: action as a result of trauma. The trauma was being told by a doctor that I wouldn't live to be forty unless I lost weight—a lot of it, and fairly quickly. I was thirty-six years old at the time.

In looking back over that period of my life, now 120 pounds lighter, fifteen clothing sizes smaller, and with almost four years behind me of maintaining my weight loss, I'm beginning to understand not just the why but, more important, the how of my accomplishment.

Every overweight person has his or her personal history of weight gain. Many of us also have histories of losing our excess weight, regaining it, losing it, and regaining it again—the pattern of cyclical dieting. I had spent my life feeling like a fat yo-yo.

I had dieted many times over a nineteen-year period, using other people's weight-loss programs and racking up one failure after another. Instead of slimming down, I ended up weighing 240 pounds. How did I finally cut the diet yo-yo string? I made the decision to lose my weight and to teach myself how to live thin for the rest of my life.

This book is the result of my experience in designing and carrying out a personal weight-management program that was a resounding and stunning success. The mark of that success is the test of time: I am still a thin woman, four years later. My weight has fluctuated a consistent 2–4 pounds, up during menstruation and down during periods of regular physical exercise. I eat the same as other normally thin people who "watch their weight." I do not think of myself as being on a diet, nor do I have fears of gaining back my weight.

What I do have is conscious knowledge, learned from personal experience, of one of the best-kept secrets of the entire $10 billion diet industry—*exactly how to stay thin for the rest of my life.*

This book is for you. If I could do it, so can you.

Getting thin, not learning how to *stay thin,* is the objective of most diet programs. Most overweighters, myself included, know how to lose weight, but it is usually to the detriment of our emotional and physical well-being, because most of us end up getting even fatter after dieting. And, as our body weight goes up, our self-esteem plummets.

I was tired of working to lose my excess weight, then struggling even harder to keep it off, and finally seeing my efforts end in failure. I wanted a diet program that would make me a winner, a success first in losing my excess fat, then in keeping it off permanently.

All my previous diets had taught me an important lesson: Nothing had really changed for me as a result of dieting, because the changes had never lasted. Before, I had dieted to rid myself of personal hurts, of feelings of shame and self-denigration. I had dieted to avoid further rejection by others and by myself. I had always begun these diets with high expectations. They had always fizzled to a quiet burp.

Always, I had dieted for loss, most obviously the loss of my excess body weight. Less obvious, but equally important, had been the desire for loss of pain, for loss of rejection, for loss of a grotesque, misshapen body. Always, I had dieted *against* something. But this time, I told myself, I would diet *for* something—gain of personal success. For me, that meant permanent weight loss.

The goal of this personal diet plan, then, is not just weight loss. The goal is to learn how to live thin from the inside out, as the body thins from the outside in. In fact, I began "living thin" even before I lost the first pound, and I continued my education through the loss of 119 more pounds, until I reached my ideal weight.

I did not begin my program with the idea of losing all my fat. My initial goal was to lose 100 pounds in six months. But ultimately I thought: Why lose only enough to live plump? Since losing weight *is* difficult (and there is no way around that fact), I figured why not go all the way down and make the hard work really worthwhile. Ultimately, the additional 20 pounds that would get me to my ideal weight seemed a molehill compared to the initial 100-pound mountain before me.

I succeeded at losing all 120 pounds in twelve months, even though I didn't know much about weight management when I began. But I learned along the way. The purpose of this book, then, is to teach you what I learned and to help you succeed, too.

The Personal Diet: A Total Weight-Management Program

Before you clean out your refrigerator and dust off your bathroom scale, let's take a look at this "personal diet." What is the rationale behind thinning from the inside out, and how does this program differ from others? What is the program's framework, and why is making it into your own personal diet essential to your success? Why is "coming to a decision" to do it so important, and what does that decision mean to you personally? Finally, will the program work for you?

The Rationale

Both my overweight history and my nineteen years of dieting have convinced me that being overweight is a personal problem that demands a personal solution if thinness, once achieved, is to be maintained permanently. The conclusions of several 1982 Columbia University studies reported in *The Canadian Journal of Public Health* support the personal-solution approach.

According to these studies, 63 percent of the overweighters who followed their own diets and changed their eating habits on their own succeeded in maintaining, on the average, a weight loss of more than 34 pounds each for a period of more than eleven years. Why does a personal-solution approach enjoy a 63-percent success rate where most popular diet programs result in a 95-percent long-term failure rate?

I believe that for most of us, being overweight stems from two personal food realities we do not share with thin people. The first is an inherent desire to overeat. It's as if the "stomach is full" switch in our bodies is permanently turned to "off," whereas in thin people the switch turns to "on" to let them know when they've eaten enough. Secondly, we have developed all kinds of food-habit patterns in an attempt to satisfy this unchecked desire to overeat.

Most popular diet programs address this second food reality by telling us merely to change our eating habits. By doing so, they claim, we automatically eliminate our desire to overeat. But does our desire to overeat really disappear along with the excess fat hugging our bodies? I don't think so.

With the help of diet behavior modification techniques, many of us have repatterned the worst of our personal food habits and indeed lost weight. Why, then, after working so hard to change our food habits, buying smaller-size clothes, and proclaiming from the rooftops how happy we are to be at our goal of splendid slenderness, do we throw away these accomplishments and begin getting fat all over again?

For more than 95 percent of us overweighters, after successful weight loss we begin to fry every food in sight, or snack our way through weekend after weekend on rich, high-calorie foods, or eat leftovers off of our mate's, our children's, even our friends' plates. The feeling of powerlessness is overwhelming as the old prediet habits come galloping back, making us gain even more weight than we lost. Why don't the changes last?

I believe the answer lies in the first food reality—the inherent, and frequent, desire to overeat. This desire, as many of you know, does not disappear with weight loss. *For some, it becomes even stronger after dieting, because it never was honestly acknowledged and subsequently changed.*

The fact is that this desire to indulge is a far greater internal force to reckon with than are the bad food habits we developed to satisfy it. Diet behavior modification experts have another name for this desire: "inner hunger." Instead of developing techniques to help us directly challenge this internal force, however, behaviorists have fixed their sights on techniques to help us change our eating habits. These techniques are based on the belief that the external environment "triggers" these habits into action, and that they are more powerful than any internal force. In other words, we can lay responsibility for our fatness on everyone but ourselves. Friends, family, coworkers, the neighborhood bakery or deli, the social environment—these are the pressure ingredients we give way to, feel victimized by, and come to believe must be changed. We do not honestly believe we have to work on changing that frequent, unchecked internal desire to overeat.

Having reached a record weight of 240 pounds, I'm the last person to deny environmental influences. Television food commercials used to go straight to my stomach. When I was a chubby little kid and padded home in tears because neighborhood kids called me "Fatty," my mother said, "Eat, you'll feel better." I did, and I grew into a fat teenager. Soon, peer pressure to be popular struck all of us. Only I struck out because my body stuck out. I went on my first diet when I was seventeen. However, the social pressure to be thin was not as strong as my internal desire to overeat. As a fat person I was tremendously influenced by my external environment. But no matter how many times I modified that environment and my food habits, my desire to overeat always won out, because the desire itself never changed. I dumped that first diet, as I did all the others over the next nineteen years, and accepted living as a fat person in a predominantly thin world.

I think of this desire running around inside us over-weighters as an undisciplined child who has been let loose in a candy store. No one knows this child better than we do. We can change the external environment and our food habits that are "triggered" by it; but unless we work simultaneously to discipline and change this internal force—thinning from the inside out, as our bodies thin from the outside in—the changes will not last.

The rationale behind the personal diet plan is this: You must be willing to learn how to master your inner desire to overeat, so that you never again feel victimized by food or by your external environment. But how, exactly, do you accomplish this?

The Framework

You can learn how to master your food desires and habits by using my program as a framework in constructing your own personal diet. The framework itself is based on realistic weight-management techniques you can tailor to your weight history, lifestyle, and food preferences. You will not want to do exactly what I did, because my personal diet was designed solely for me; yours must be structured specifically for you.

For example, I was 120 pounds overweight. I'm single, live alone, and grew up eating meat and potatoes. You, on the other hand, may be 20 or 35 pounds overweight, married or a single parent, and responsible for feeding growing children.

And perhaps you grew up eating fish, pasta, chili, or curry dishes.

What we do have in common, and what makes this program applicable to all of us, however, is the fact that we share an unchecked desire to overeat and fat food habits that support that desire. I designed this program to confront, to challenge, and to replace both of these fat food realities with thin ones.

I based the framework for this program on my personal dieting experiences and a lifetime of fat self-knowledge. In order to make the program work for you, you must be willing to actively participate and to base your diet on your self-knowledge and food preferences. Remember, if I can do it, you can, too.

Now, let's take a look at the program's three working principles.

Principle No. 1: Your Personal Commitment

Your decision to follow the program represents a personal commitment to yourself to learn *how to stay thin,* not just how to get thin. Although it sounds hard to believe, it is a resolve you can live with for the rest of your life.

Principle No. 2: Your Thinning Perspective

Getting started in your program does not mean immediately reducing your calorie intake. Once you've made your decision, you begin to develop a "thinning perspective" that directly challenges your desire to overeat, and you acquire the necessary personal diet tactics and tools you will use first in losing weight, then in maintaining the weight loss.

These personal diet tactics and tools include techniques to counter your overeating desire's resistance to change; basic measurement tools like a scale, a full-length mirror, and a tape measure, as well as charts for recording changes about to take

10

place; and specific food suggestions for losing weight and permanent maintenance of your ideal weight.

Principle No. 3: Reducing Your Calorie Intake

Your personal food-plan diet will teach you how to eliminate many of the calories in the foods you've been eating most of your life. Equally important, you will also learn how to maintain a sense of physical and emotional well-being during all three phases of the plan.

The Three-Phase Personal Food-Plan Diet

Depending on which calorie plan you follow (I have included in the appendix my own menu plans for 800, 1000, and 1200 calories daily), you can expect to lose on the average 6–10 pounds per month. I lost 120 pounds in twelve months following a medically approved 800-calorie plan.

The three phases of the personal food-plan diet are as follows:

During Phase One, you will learn how to replace certain familiar foods—the foods you've been eating most of your life that are responsible for those unwanted pounds—with other familiar foods that will instead take pounds off and keep them off. Although you will have reached at least one-third of your weight-loss goal at the conclusion of Phase One, you will probably experience feelings of boredom and tiredness, which may erode your resolve. That's why the personal food-plan diet has a second phase.

During Phase Two, you will learn how to get through the serious dieter's dilemma, "the diet mentality," with its accompanying undermining feelings of boredom and tiredness. You replace these "dump the diet" attitudes with your "thinning perspective," which enables you to lose the other two-thirds of your excess weight. At the conclusion of Phase Two you will have reached your ideal weight.

You will not stop the program the minute you reach this goal. Remember, the personal diet is a *total* weight-management program. During Phase Three, your weight-loss-maintenance phase, you learn two crucial things: how to overcome the very real fear of weight regain, and how to live thin emotionally.

Living Thin and the Role of Exercise

The last element of the program's framework is the role played by physical exercise. It was very hard for me to give exercise a healthy, consistent role in my life, but I did eventually win the struggle. Exercise *can* play an important role for you during your weight loss, but I found that I was able to lose my weight without exercising. However, without the regular physical exercise I now schedule into my life *when needed,* I could not continue to be a healthy, thin person.

Will This Program Work for You?

This program offers a great deal more than a weight-reduction plan: it teaches you how to *live thin.* The first step is to come to a decision to do so. But what does that decision mean to you personally?

In order to become thin permanently, you will need an inner strength no one else can give you or regiment into you. This inner strength is not willpower, nor is it a capacity to discipline your desire to eat whatever you want whenever you want it. The source of your inner strength is *self-honesty.*

Self-honesty is your personal guide to permanent weight loss. In coming to your decision to follow this program, if you are being honest with yourself when you say, "Yes, I really want to get thin and stay thin, not just try it, but do it," you will succeed.

CHAPTER TWO

Coming to a Decision

I DO NOT COME FROM a fat family. Although my mother gained weight after I was born, my father and two elder brothers had always been lean and handsome. We were an average middle-class family who ate bacon and eggs for breakfast, meat and potatoes for dinner, and occasionally spaghetti on Friday nights. I ate second helpings of almost everything, thirds on spaghetti because it was such fun to eat. I liked to eat.

As a preadolescent, I was happy. My brothers were embarrassed for me, but they didn't like me any less because I was fat. My friends didn't like me any less either, until we passed puberty and practically everyone started paying attention to their bodies. I'd always been aware of being overweight because the neighborhood kids reminded me of that fact often enough. My parents tried to salve my hurts by telling me, "Sticks and stones may break your bones, but names like 'Fatty' can never hurt you." They were wrong.

Teenage boys didn't call me names. They just ignored me. That's what hurt. I didn't like being rejected just because of my chunky body. "What about the person inside that body?" I wanted to cry out. My girl friends were asked out on dates. I wasn't. All they talked about every Monday morning was what a great time they'd had over the weekend. Staying home and watching television didn't begin to compare with the glamour,

13

the romance, and the high adventures my friends were having. I began to feel left out. Something terribly important seemed to be going on in everyone's life but my own.

I went on my first diet in order to lose weight and join the crowd. I didn't like being hurt, and I liked being excluded even less. I soon got bored, however, eating boiled eggs, broiled hamburger, and low-fat cottage cheese every day. I wanted to eat greasy hamburgers, french fries, milkshakes, and candy bars, just like everyone else. Since I'd developed a second-helping habit, I missed that, too.

When boyfriends failed to appear out of air thinner than I, I lost patience with my diet and quit. Interestingly, I felt more hurt and rejected when I was slimmer than I had when I was fat. Not surprisingly, I promptly regained the 20 pounds it had taken me two months to lose. There is no question that food met expectations for me that people did not.

There were other diets as I got older. And more failures. The more I tried to lose weight, the harder it became. My metabolism rebelled, and the task of shedding even 10 pounds became not only arduous but torturous, because it seemed to take forever. I lost more patience than weight.

In emotional desperation and physical exhaustion, I turned to the fad diets that promised instant weight loss effortlessly. All I had to provide was the desire to slim down. These diet programs provided everything else. I passively followed the rigid control systems these diets set up, and as long as I adhered to them I did lose weight. I was told what to eat, when to eat it, in what quantity, and even how to eat it. Unfortunately, they did not address the issue of life *after* weight loss. So, each time I quit one of these programs, I also quit the control system responsible for the weight loss.

I'm talking about programs like the following:

• cheater's diet: you have the willpower to hold out until you can binge again

- drinking person's diet: you drink your calories instead of eat them
- exercise-through-sex diet: "reach for your mate" instead of a plate
- one-day-a-week-fasting diet: you empty your body before you stuff it
- single-food-elimination diet: you eat all the protein and fat you want and eliminate carbohydrates; or you fill up on carbohydrates and exclude fat and animal proteins (like meat and dairy products)

The problem with these diets isn't so much in the weight loss itself, my doctor told me in 1981, but in the nutritional imbalances such diets can cause. For me, however, the real problem was that I continued with the fad diets, adding to my list of failures.

I did lose weight on these diets, sometimes lots of it. But I always gained it back plus more, which ensured that I'd soon be following yet another fad diet. The diet made the decisions for me of what to eat and how, until I rebelled, made my own decisions, and promptly got fat again. My willpower was always stronger than their rules. The problem for me was that my willpower, after years of dieting, knew only how to gain weight.

By 1973 I was no longer fat. I was obese, weighing close to 200 pounds. I had finished graduate school and spent half a year looking for a teaching job. Everyone turned me down for a job. I was advised not to take my failure personally, though: there were simply too many teachers for too few jobs; a glut on the market, they called it. I knew it was my stomach, only it was called gluttony.

When I went home to the West Coast after my failed job search on the East Coast, my life seemed to come to a standstill. I began living off my savings and fell into a daily routine that I came to despise almost as much as I despised myself. For six months I got up every morning and padded into the kitchen to make a huge breakfast. Then I carried everything into the living room, turned on the television, and plopped myself onto the couch (usually in a prone position). I would stay that way all day except for excursions back into the kitchen to replenish my food supply.

Occasionally I cried, but my tears weren't from watching a sad scene on TV. They were the result of seeing my life pass away on that couch in a curtain-drawn room day after day.

I wasn't even thirty years old, but my life seemed over. I wasn't getting better as I got older. I was just getting fatter. Instead of lots of friends, I now had a telephone that never rang; restaurants, movie theaters, and weekend parties I didn't get invited to; and clothing stores I could not shop in because nothing would fit.

In early 1974 I tried another popular diet, this one low in carbohydrates. I gave up bread, potatoes, pasta, and other high-starch foods, and ate small portions of meat, poultry, eggs, and dairy products. The diet was strictly regimented. So too was my resolve to lose weight, along with my feelings of sadness, extreme loneliness, and self-dislike because I was betraying myself.

I wanted to work and to begin having a social life. I also wanted to be loved and found attractive by a man. And I wanted to like myself again, to restore my self-respect and personal dignity, both of which seemed to have taken up permanent residence in my refrigerator. If I could just lose weight, I told myself, all my problems would be solved.

I did lose weight. I went down to 150 pounds and a tight size 14. I got a job teaching literature and composition at a small university in Illinois, and I thrived on the mental gymnastics of my work. My colleagues respected my professional competence. I respected my physical accomplishments. I believed that everything important to me in my life had finally come together. I was wrong.

I was failing to make friends. Although I was accepted professionally, I did not feel accepted personally. So, I turned back to my nightly full stomach for consolation. Even before I received notice from the university that budget cuts had eliminated my job, I had begun to gain weight again. My fantasy of

16

being magically transformed from fat to slim overnight had not been realized, nor had my hopes for romance, genuine acceptance, or lasting self-respect. I was still the pretty face attached to an overweight body. I never made it to thinness in body or mind. My desire once again burned out before my fat burned off. Then, I had neither the solace of a full stomach nor the comfort of good friends.

Teaching positions were scarce, and being overweight sealed my fate. I left Illinois and returned again to the West Coast. I also changed professions and started my own business as a literary agent, based in California. I did not believe my personal appearance was what counted in the publishing business; exciting, new writers and their work did. And many of them were based in California, as I was.

I was determined to make something of my life now. I did not want to return to spending my days lying on my couch in a darkened room, eating my way through one happy television show after another. Getting out into the real world and working were much more exciting and a great deal less lonely, at least during the day.

I loved my new work and became totally absorbed in it. The phone rang constantly. I dined out frequently with clients and with editors visiting from New York. There were more invitations to book parties, publishing conferences, and professional-association dinner parties than I had time to attend.

I was so caught up in being pursued for my professional services that this kind of attention temporarily supplanted my need for the other—that of being pursued for myself. I felt personally invisible to others, and I began to grow more invisible to myself as I added more poundage day by day. Finally one day it occurred to me that I seemed unconcerned about the growing state of my body. Although I could have reacted with relief, I didn't, because I realized that I had simply stopped feeling anything that concerned me personally—good or bad. Since my natural protective instincts were no longer functioning, I knew something was up, and it wasn't just my weight.

One day in early 1981, I returned from clothes shopping,

in preparation for an upcoming business trip to New York, having purchased clothes in size 22. I came into my house, put the packages on the table, and set my ponderous body down on my couch. I sank into sighs of self-pity and sadness as I recalled the last shopping expedition and the clothes purchased in size 20.

Buying clothes had always been a traumatic experience. Even when I shopped for smaller sizes after dieting, the sizes were never small enough to meet my expectations. And now they were even bigger. The only time I'd ever grown beyond size 20 before, back in 1974, I'd gone on a diet and reversed the trend. What was happening to me now, I asked myself, that I hadn't reversed it this time?

Although my business had been steadily picking up, my spirits had been steadily going down, and on that cold day in January 1981, they hit rock bottom. With a self-honesty I'd grown accustomed to eating myself away from, I stopped remembering prior sadnesses and disappointments and began thinking instead of my current personal life and how empty it really was. I not only had no love life, I no longer had real expectations of ever having one.

The tears finally came, not silently, but with great racking sobs. I cried for what seemed like hours. When I blew my nose one last time and wiped away the tears, I looked about me and realized that the sun had set. I turned on the light next to the couch and looked at my body through clear eyes.

The body I saw was even more shocking than the size-22 clothes I had just purchased to cover it. I had eaten my way into this morbidly obese state all by myself. There was no one else to blame. Although I was mentally and emotionally exhausted, I sat there on that couch and let myself know just how fat I was. I didn't ask myself why or even how I had reached 200 pounds again. I just let myself feel the fat from my cheeks to the tops of my feet. I let myself feel with my hands the mounds of flab covering every rotund inch of me.

I reluctantly but honestly admitted that my weight problem was no one's fault but my own. I could no longer blame even the fad diets for failing to help me, I had wanted to lose weight and I had done so. What I hadn't wanted to do was to give up my desire to overeat. I knew then that I had to find a way to change this desire, or I would end up eating myself to death.

This pronouncement scared the hell out of me. I wanted to race into my kitchen like a banshee and throw out every food in sight. I never wanted to eat again; I wanted to starve myself and this horrid desire to overeat. I had experienced such over-zealous, unrealistic urgings in the past, usually accompanied by feelings of remorse, guilt, or shame. But I refused the inner urging this time. Instead, I boldly took a hard look at this "fat self" part of me that dwelled inside my overweight body and was prompting that urging. This is what I saw.

A "thought" would pop into my head to eat something when I wasn't even hungry, or, for that matter, when I wasn't anywhere near a food that I usually desired. Or, I would be standing in front of my fridge with the intent of gathering salad fixings on a hot summer day. Instead, I would open the door and reach for the highest-calorie food in sight, even though I couldn't have been rebelling from a diet since I hadn't been thinking "diet" when I thought "salad." But whenever I did contemplate reducing, I would hear this "whisper" in my ear: "I really want to eat whatever I want whenever I want it."

Then I understood that, whenever I actually was dieting, the suggesting thoughts became insatiable cravings; and I responded as though to incessant marching orders to procure high-calorie food and plenty of it. The whispers in my ear became command orders to either maintain the status quo of my overweight body or to gain even more weight at all costs. I had unconsciously accepted this as a normal part of dieting. Indeed, weight gain after dieting was "secretly" anticipated.

Sitting on my couch on that cold day in January 1981, I finally exposed that "secret" part of me behind the thoughts, intentions, and anticipations of eating with abandon. I was genuinely surprised to find this sneaky, clever, and tyrannical part of me. I had never before understood why my sincere efforts to lose weight went down to defeat over and over again, while I got fatter and fatter. I was beginning to understand now.

19

My fortress of fatness had once worked for me. It had kept away from me the people and the pain of living. I felt safe. With my self-protection expressed in the form of insulating layers of fat, I felt that I had closed out the problems of living. Inadvertently, I had also closed out its joys. My fortress had become a prison. I was the victim of my emotional self-protection. Others still couldn't get in. I could not get out. No wonder all my previous diet efforts had gone down to defeat: I had never lost the tyrannical desire to overeat as my principal protection against emotional pain.

Stunned by my first moment of fat recognition, I sat there on my couch and let myself know exactly how fat I was. But what was I going to do about it?

The answer was to do three things: lose the fat, change the desire and the food habits developed to feed the desire, and develop a healthy emotional-protection system that my desire to overeat could not invade and take over. I knew how to lose the fat and how to change my food habits. I had no idea how to change that powerful internal desire. I did not know any alternative responses to unpleasant feelings other than to eat my way through them.

I wanted to do everything that very day. But wanting to change and knowing how were not the same thing. I did not want to risk another failed attempt. Unfortunately, this wasn't to be my last bout with fatness. While searching for workable answers, I went through still another desperate time during which all my failures loomed up at me. (In retrospect, I realized that at that time in my life I was still learning all the issues I would have to confront before finally coming to a decision that would stick.)

I did go to New York in my size-22 clothes, and trudged around Manhattan feeling people's stares. I felt like a caricature, as wide as I was tall. My polyester blouses stretched tighter and tighter across a stomach that just kept getting bigger as I ate my way through my embarrassment. I felt that people were snickering as I pushed through the subway turnstiles, literally squeezing through sideways, holding my stomach up, lifting it over the top as the turnstile wheeled me through.

I came home physically exhausted, emotionally debilitated, and fat enough to burst the seams of my size-22 clothes. By August I had shot up to a size 26 and tipped the scale at 240 pounds. Clearly, since January, that fat-self part of me had been showing off its power to resist change.

Yet, despite my additional 40-pound weight gain and my awareness of just how powerful this destructive internal desire really was, I still wanted to change. I was determined to find the *how* of change. I did not believe the singular solution was dieting. For me, it had been nothing but a battleground for constantly saying "no" to the temptation to overeat. At 240 pounds, what I needed was a way to say "yes" to my desire to live thin. But how?

The answer to this question, and to many others I'd been seeking for nine months, finally came in late August, when I had dinner with my friends Dr. Roger Wilson and his wife, Nancy, who is a registered dietitian. That evening, we discussed my weight problem after they observed that I had gained about 15 pounds in the four weeks since they had last seen me.

Dr. Wilson confirmed for me what I already knew but refused to admit: my physical health was in imminent danger because of the stress of 240 pounds hanging on my small body frame. He suggested that I go on an 800-calorie diet of balanced, nutritious meals I could put together myself—in other words, a personal food-plan diet. He also recommended an over-the-counter vitamin-mineral tablet. He said that if I really changed my eating habits and used basic dieting tools (like scales, a full-length mirror, a food log, and a calorie counter), he believed I could lose 100 pounds in six months!

But counting calories and changing my eating habits were the *how of becoming thin*. They were not the *how of staying thin*; such a diet plan would not teach me how to live thin. I did not want to count calories or to be on a diet for the rest of my life. I did not want to fall into the diet-mentality trap of losing all my excess weight only to discover that I had not learned how, on the way down, to stay thin. I wanted to diet, but at the same time I wanted to learn how to *live thin* forever.

For the first time in my life, I felt like I was using my head instead of my stomach to come to grips with my weight problem. For the past nine months I had been a passive, ineffectual listener to and observer of my warring food desires, unable to gain control of one or strengthen the other. And as long as I remained passive, I was the victim of my desire to eat whatever I wanted whenever I wanted it *regardless of the consequences.* And the consequence of my overweight life thus far was that I lived in a pain-infested prison of self-imposed fatness.

I had to break out of that prison, but not just to stop the pain. I wanted to feel joy, to restore my self-respect, to take back the dignity my fatness had robbed from me. Most of all, I wanted to take back the freedom to actively make my own choices, not passively follow those of my internal fat self. In coming to my decision to plan a personal diet program that would teach me how to live thin, I realized that I would have to make a conscious choice, and keep making that choice *over and over again,* between continuing to live fat or actively starting to live thin.

Dr. Wilson's final advice to me was: "Don't just try it. Do it." It took me only a moment to consider the alternative.

With the knowledge I had been gaining about myself over the past nine months, since that gloomy day when I reached 200 pounds and then gained another 40 on top of it, I realized that learning how to live thin would actually be easier than continuing to live fat. What gave me the strength to come to my "yes" decision was tapping into the new self-honesty that had begun on that cold day back in January.

Being honest about what I wanted to eat would no longer mean frequent self-indulgences. Being honest now meant being consciously aware of either actively choosing to stay fat and unhappy, or actively choosing to slim down and stay that way.

I began to see that this was a mental process as well as a physical one. *Thinking* about the decisions I would have to make the rest of my life, then actively *making* them, I was in fact *"living thin" before I lost the first fat pound.* That's what I set out to do when I came to my decision, and that's what I accomplished in carrying it out.

In making my decision, I went through a series of steps. You will have to come to your own decision, but the steps that you will go through will be the same as mine:

1. *Acknowledge the two food realities of your overweight body:* the desire to overeat, and the food habits supporting that desire.
2. *Express the willingness to confront your "secret" desire to overeat* and acknowledge responsibility for that desire and its effect on your body.
3. *Allow yourself to honestly feel the genuine desire to change,* do not just wishfully think about it.
4. *Be honest enough with yourself to admit* that not changing is a far more painful and difficult way to live than actively choosing to live your life as a thin person with choices you otherwise would not have.
5. *Actively use your self-honesty as a form of internal strength* with which to make the choice to live thin, and be willing to do so for the rest of your life.

You cannot expect the process of coming to your decision to be easy or painless. On the other hand, in thinking about going through these steps, it may help you, as it did me, to consider the alternative.

In contemplating this process, you may be asking yourself right now if, like me, you will take nine months to get through it and gain weight in the interim. I do not believe you will.

Remember, I spent a lot of that nine months just figuring out *how* to change, formulating the blueprint for this program.

You have your own self-honesty to guide you in making the choices that will ensure your physical and emotional well-being, but you also have me as your personal guide toward permanent weight loss. You will not be going through this program alone. Further, I will recommend specific things for you to do at various points along the way that I either did, or did not do and wished I had, or that I did later in the program and wished I had done sooner.

A personal weight-management program is effective only

23

when you make the commitment to permanent weight loss. To help you make that commitment and say "yes" to your desire to live thin, ask yourself the following questions, and answer them honestly. You will be tempted to answer "no" to some of them. At that moment of temptation, you will be faced with a conscious choice. Let your self-honesty guide you in making the choice that's right for you.

1. Are you genuinely ready to experience your fatness, to look in the mirror long enough or to feel with your hands just how much of you there is, and not run away from the encounter right afterward?
2. Can you hear the faint stirrings of a real desire to change?
3. Can you hear the ominous rumblings of that part of you that is preventing you from starting your own program by predicting failure; telling you that it's just too hard; that you don't have the patience; insisting that you can't live without "certain foods"; or saying it's just too complicated for you?
4. Are you tired of dieting to lose?
5. Are you ready to diet to gain personal success?
6. Can you recognize that part of you inside your over-weight body that will try to rob you of any success and turn any weight loss into failure?
7. Are you ready to actively and repeatedly choose to help your desire for permanent thinness to emerge from the inside out while your body thins from the outside in?

CHAPTER THREE

Getting Started

ONCE YOU HAVE MADE THE commitment to learn how to live thin, you will not immediately begin reducing calories and saying "no" to your desire to overeat. It's my opinion that your "desire" could overpower you and defeat you before you've even begun to carry out your commitment. Remember, losing weight is only part of your total weight-management program. The other part is learning to live thin, and you begin doing that even before you lose the first fat pound.

Learning to live thin begins with initiating a "thinning perspective" toward your two food desires, which you do in coming to your decision. You then continue developing this perspective by creating a supportive environment for controlling your desire to overeat and for strengthening your desire to learn to live thin.

This means that you will now begin taking the time to think with your head rather than through your stomach in dealing with food desires. You will use this "diet preparation time" to do the following:

- *Watch yourself.* Observe and discover the principal characteristics of your two opposing food desires.
- *Watch other people.* Observe and discover characteris-

tics of other peoples' food desires, especially the ones that help keep thin people thin.

- *Create a supportive environment.* Get medical and family support; decide whether to tell your friends and co-workers; find a pal to diet with.
- *Defat your food environment.* As you remove your favorite fat foods from your kitchen, observe your desire to overeat and listen to your internal squeal of horror.
- *Recognize that hereditary fatness is not forever.* Face the facts of fat genes, a "fat metabolism," and the soundness of the energy equation (to lose weight, you must consume fewer calories than you burn).

Let's now go through each of these activities and look more closely at the process of developing your thinning perspective.

Watch Yourself

In coming to your decision, you will have gained enough familiarity with your opposing food desires to make a "yes" choice in favor of your thin one. In order to continue making this choice, however, you must gain more knowledge about both desires. The self-knowledge you glean in observing and discovering their principal daily characteristics, and the way in which you glean that knowledge, will help develop your thinning perspective.

First, turn your attention to observing your desires for food. *Listen* to your thoughts about what you want to eat, when, and how you want it to taste. Listen for comments such as "needs a touch of mustard" or "not enough butter." When you hear "I want something sweet" and immediately think "candy bar" or "homemade chocolate-chip cookies," replace these food images with "fresh sliced apple" or "a bowl of fresh berries sprinkled with cinnamon" and observe what happens.

In addition to listening to your thoughts about food, you must learn to discriminate between the voices of your desires.

For example, you may consider your desire for butter perfectly "normal" when looking at a baked potato. On the other hand, if you are tuning into your desire to lose weight, while making a chicken sandwich you may hear a little internal voice say, "Hold the mayo, needs a touch of mustard instead." These are two very different voices. Consciously become aware of which voice of desire you want to encourage. Butter and mayonnaise each have approximately 100 calories per tablespoon. It's my belief that you may not know the calorie content of what you are about to eat, but your "secret" desire to overeat does know.

For example, if you have dieted before, think back to your attitude toward some of the foods you ate while dieting: raw vegetables, low-fat cottage cheese, or half a grapefruit. You probably thought of these strictly as diet foods and sighed in boredom before eating them. Now ask yourself what gave you the idea that they were only diet foods, never to be eaten unless you were dieting. Many thin people eat foods in the low calorie range all the time and don't think twice about it. On the other hand, overweighters do think twice, and sometimes both resent and resist eating such foods. Where does this diet-mentality attitude come from?

As your diet-mentality attitudes begin to surface into your awareness, you may want to berate yourself for being fat-sighted. Don't. It is not you who have erred. It is only a small part of you that is manipulating you into resisting the low-calorie-range foods, instead demanding foods in the higher ranges, and plenty of them.

Most people do not like to make changes, especially in matters of food preference. Being overweight, you prefer the kinds of foods that keep you fat. When you focus on the internal force behind your preferences and habits, you can observe that small but powerful part of you I have been calling "the fat-self desire."

As you may recall, one of my early difficulties in observing my internal desire to overeat was that I did not know what to do with the knowledge I gained. The answer I discovered was a technique fiction writers often use.

I decided that the real star of my program was not going to

be me, my body, or my fat food habits. Instead, it would be that "secret" food desire inside me—the one thing about me that had never changed during previous diets. While its effects were visible to me and everyone else, the desire itself remained invisible, deeply embedded in my negative thoughts and feelings about myself as a fat person. I did not believe I could permanently change this desire unless I could somehow "see" it. That meant bringing it to the surface of my conscious awareness, all the time realizing that this desire was only *one part* of me, not *all* of me. I may have looked fat on the outside, but I knew deep down there was something else there than pure fat.

To make my internal fat desire visible to me, I literally invented a rotund little character. I gave it all the characteristics that I had come to understand while coming to my decision. As my diet program took shape, I added to the character's personality by observing its actions and reactions to food. I even gave it a name: my Fat Self.

The first thing I wanted to do with my Fat Self was to wrap my hands around its fat little neck and shake it from head to toe the way the fat on my body shook every time I moved. But this tyrannical Fat Self was not the enemy. It was an errant, out-of-control part of me that I had blithely ignored and refused to acknowledge responsibility for. In fact, I had become blind to it.

As I began developing my thinning perspective, I knew that I needed compassion, not anger, toward this part of me. I did not believe I would lose my Fat Self along with my fat, and I had no intention of becoming an angry thin woman constantly beating myself up for once having been fat. The kind of permanent change I was after would not come out of anger or fear. Those were the ways of my Fat Self.

To help me counter those ways, I invented another little character counterpart to it: my Thin Self. I attributed to it all the characteristics of my other internal food desire—that part of me that honestly wanted to slim down and stay that way.

These were not Laurel and Hardy–type characters acting

28

out performances of "it's all in good fun, gang!" They were food desires almost totally opposite in purpose, expressed in my thoughts, feelings, and actions toward food.

This is what they sounded like arguing whenever food or thoughts of it were close at hand:

"I don't really want a second helping." *Oh yes you do.*

"I'm too tired to do anything." *Eat, you'll feel better.*

"I wonder if I can eat just one cookie." *Of course you can. Just eat one at a time.*

"I think I'll eat a light lunch today because I'm not very hungry." *Good, you can make up for it at dinner.*

This is how I pictured my internal characters:

My Fat Self was accustomed always to getting its way. It was smug, conceited, and full of the false pride that comes from constant abuse of power in will and appetite, both of which it controls exceptionally well. It had a volatile temper, lashing out at my weak little Thin Self one minute, grouchy the next, then going off to sulk on massive cushions of adipose tissue. It left in its wake feelings of guilt, doubt, and angst, which strengthened my Thin Self's sense of failure and vulnerability. In other words, my Fat Self looked exactly like the pompous, overweight dictator I knew it to be.

My Thin Self, which I knew slightly from previous diets, also had a temper, but it was not destructive or unreasonable. There was genuine humility there, but it was more realistic. My Thin Self did not manipulate me into believing I wanted more food when I didn't honestly want it. On the contrary, my Thin Self within wanted a thin body. I couldn't visualize my Thin Self, however, because I had never been thin. But I believed that it looked like the reverse of my Fat Self.

Try to visualize your fat food desire, using the characteristics you have been observing and discovering. Then try to picture a second little character, based on the knowledge you've

29

gained in observing your desire for thinness. You, the director of your desires, observing them in food performance, will soon begin actively to redirect them.

During this preparation time, continue "studying" your characters. You are setting the stage for change. You must look within to determine the appropriate attitude for yourself. Will it be the same old diet-mentality attitude, or will it be a newly developing compassionate and realistic thinning perspective? As the director of your internal food desires, you must make this choice, not that small part of you that has made and kept you overweight.

Watch Other People

You are no longer a "forever fat" person. That awareness alone makes people-watching all the more important, and the information you glean from observing others can help you learn how to do things differently. Equally important are the feelings and attitudes you should bring to this new activity of people-watching. Instead of using your observation of others to feel guilt, envy, shame, or false pride, use it as an opportunity for your Thin Self to speak up and be heard.

1. Pay particular attention to how people eat, comparing thin people with overweighters. Emulate the former.
2. Talk to thin people about not only what they eat but how. What do they do the week after feasting, or the week before taking a vacation? Ask them especially about desserts, how they eat them and still remain thin.

I recall going to a small dinner party during my preparation time. The occasion was to feast on fresh albacore caught by my hosts. I discovered something very important that night.

There were five of us present, three of us very overweight, the other two at normal body weight. The moment we sat down for hors d'oeuvres—fresh raw vegetables, four kinds of cheese (two of them soft and creamy), and a variety of crackers, party breads, and little cakes—my perception of myself changed.

I ate only what the thin woman sitting next to me ate. Together, we finished the fresh vegetables. She ate only one piece of cheese—the hard kind—and without bread or a cracker. I asked her why she didn't eat more cheese.

"We haven't even had dinner yet," she said, "and I have to watch my weight. I could nibble on all that cheese endlessly without even thinking about the calories adding up."

I didn't have a second piece of cheese. However, my overweight friends feasted on the breads and cheeses, finishing them all before we went in to dinner.

As I sat down at the dinner table that night, it was not as a morbidly obese woman; it was as a thinning woman, watching my weight and emulating my new role model.

I valued the knowledge I gained both about myself and others that night. Observation alone, however, without also talking with the people you're watching, can be very misleading. Most thin people do occasionally eat rich, high-calorie foods. But how often do they do so, and what adjustments do they make in their diets to compensate for the additional calories?

Then there are those thin people who have to eat large quantities just to keep skin on their bones. When you run into one of them, by all means envy them, but don't try to learn from them. They have nothing to teach you.

You can learn from others, but your Fat Self is your best teacher. Your Fat Self means well, and it will try to help—its way. Appreciate its efforts, but don't follow its advice. When you cannot hear your Thin Self, pursue the opposite of your Fat Self's suggestions. Above all, don't torture yourself. You are developing a personal diet program that will help you to grow emotionally while losing weight physically, and enable you to live thin forever. Your program is not a punishment for having gotten fat in the first place. The more you realize this, the more successful you will be in developing your thinning perspective.

Create a Supportive Environment

Developing a thinning perspective to eventually replace your Fat Self's diet mentality is not a small undertaking. Many of your feelings about food reflect your feelings about yourself. When you begin changing your attitudes toward food, you may think you are changing your entire personality. You are not; you are changing only that small part of you that wants to keep your body overweight.

Nonetheless, your fears of change, magnified by your Fat Self's fears, can make it difficult emotionally to get started on your program. Therefore, it's important to create a reassuring and emotionally supportive environment around you. Your doctor, family, friends, and co-workers can help you lessen your fears and can encourage you in the constructive, healthful program you are initiating.

Your Doctor

See your doctor for a check-up and a recommendation for the total number of calories you should eat daily to lose weight without endangering your health. Most diets come in 700, 800, 1000, 1200, even 1500-calorie plans. Do not go below 1200 calories per day without medical supervision, as it could endanger your health.

Your doctor can also help you determine the following:

- *Special dietary needs.* Are you diabetic or hypertensive, or do you have high cholesterol levels, and what modifications in specific food items should you make in planning your personal food menus?
- *Multiple vitamin-mineral tablet.* Should you take one daily to supplement the nutrients in your diet plan?
- *Your ideal weight.* What is the realistic range for your ideal weight, considering your gender, age, cyclical dieting history, height, and body-frame size?

- *Adequate weight-loss time.* What is a realistic amount of time you can expect to take to reach your ideal weight?
- *Exercise recommendations.* Are there specific kinds of physical exercise you should avoid, and others that would be quite safe for you?

See your doctor *before* you start dieting. Your personal diet should take into account the needs of your temperament and your lifestyle, your food preferences, and your nutritional requirements. Equally important, your doctor can ensure that your medical needs are filled. He or she can be one of the most important people in your support system.

Family Support

Tell your family what you are doing and how you are thinning from the inside out. Be careful not to blame them for the existence of your Fat Self. Do not allow them to tempt your Fat Self beyond your control.

If some or all of your family members are overweight, you might want to encourage them to go through the personal diet program with you. If your family members are thin, ask them for their support and patience while you catch up with them.

If you have been overfeeding yourself, you may also have been overfeeding your children. For a sound discussion of child nutrition, I recommend that you read *Jane Brody's Nutrition Book* (see appendix B).

If your family members are openly nonsupportive, listen carefully to what they have to say. Their voices are the echoes of your Fat Self. Examples of nonsupportiveness are as follows:

"You've gone on diets so many times and ended up fatter than before. I wonder how fat you're going to be this time."

"You can go on a diet if you want, but don't expect me to change the way I eat. I still want my five-course dinners, snacks, and cold beer in the fridge."

"But we like you fat. There's so much there to love."

How do you deal with such attitudes in your own home?

You don't. You can change your Fat Self, but you cannot change the world and everyone else in it.

There can also be more subtle forms of nonsupport from your family. A classic example is the mother who brags openly to all her friends about how her grown child is successfully losing weight, then invites her child over for lavish, "lovingly" prepared meals consisting exclusively of extremely high-calorie foods.

Another example is the spouse who responds to your announcement of a recent 10-pound loss with, "That's wonderful. Let's go out to dinner to celebrate."

You can deal with these subtle underminings of your intentions and your accomplishments by gently but firmly refusing to accept them. Tell your mother you appreciate her encouragement but cannot eat the meals she's prepared. Then, don't eat them. Tell your spouse you're delighted that he or she wants to help you celebrate your weight loss, then suggest a form of celebrating that doesn't involve calories.

Should You Tell Your Friends and Co-Workers?

I decided to tell my friends, but for the wrong reason. I did not go to them for encouragement, but instead sought their approval and acceptance of me as a thin person before I was in fact thin. This was an unrealistic expectation I put upon them, and added pressure I put upon myself. I was indeed beginning to live thin from the inside out, but my body was not yet thinning from the outside in.

When I announced my personal diet plan, I did not see the trap Fat Self was setting for me.

"How many diets have you been on, Elizabeth?"

"Don't get your hopes up too high."

"That's an awful lot of weight to lose."

"Isn't that what's called a crash diet? I thought you had more sense than that!"

I was disappointed in my friends' skeptical responses. Instead of helping me relieve the pressure I was feeling—my Fat

Self trying to deny that I had any real hope for success—my friends had inadvertently added to it.

They had also reminded me of the difficult time I was having emotionally. I now had the pressures of a busy social life and my new literary agency. My friends felt that this wasn't the time for me to begin a new diet.

I wavered. My Thin Self won out. Now *was* the time to begin my own diet program. Being overweight closed out my choices to live as I wanted to live; according to my doctor, to live at all.

Going to my friends right after coming to my decision to diet had been a mistake, but I later corrected it by going back to them after I'd begun losing weight, and this time seeking their encouragement, not their approval or acceptance. Acceptance of myself as a thin person could only come from me.

In deciding whether to tell your own friends and co-workers during preparation time, keep in mind the following:

1. Seek their encouragement, not their approval or acceptance.
2. Be selective about whom you tell. Some friends and co-workers, like family members, may be more supportive than others.
3. Above all, be guided by your feelings and experiences, not the impatience or unrealistic expectations of your Fat Self.

Find a Pal to Diet With

The buddy system may give you much-needed strength at your weakest, fat-tempting moments. I believe that sharing your successes and joys with someone who "knows" adds double doses of growing strength to your Thin Self.

Finally, the gift of giving—of sharing, with another overweight person, your knowledge, your experiences, and your feelings while going through the three phases of your personal food-plan diet—is truly an act of your Thin Self. Your Fat Self knows only how to take, and never for your benefit.

Defat Your Food Environment

You do want to acknowledge and respect the strength of your Fat Self. However, this does not mean offering your Fat Self the wide array of high-calorie foods you normally keep stocked in your kitchen, your car, or your office.

Remove these outrageous temptations from your environment. If members of your family protest, patiently ask them to stop supporting your Fat Self at least through the duration of your first phase and the loss of at least one-third of your excess weight.

If you're not sure exactly which foods to remove, ask yourself the following questions and listen for your Fat Self's answer:

1. When you eat for emotional hunger and comfort, which foods do you consistently reach for?
2. Which foods do you tell yourself you buy for drop-in visitors but honestly buy for yourself?
3. Can you drink alcohol moderately and then also eat moderately?
4. How many "sweet teeth" do you really have?

Remove the tempting foods from your environment immediately. You may have to bodily throw them out of your house, your car, or your desk at work. Don't forget to wave goodbye.

Do not be alarmed at the thought that you will have no "real" food left in your life once you remove the tempting items. That thought is only your Fat Self cunningly trying to dissuade you from carrying out this operation.

Recognize That Hereditary Fatness Is Not Forever

Genetic Factors In Your Heredity

Do you come from an overweight family? Do you believe your excess weight is due to your genes rather than to your eating habits, your lifestyle, and your well-fed desire for more? According to Ray Hodgson and Peter Miller, authors of *Self-Watching: Addictions, Habits, Compulsions: What to Do About Them*, there is no conclusive scientific evidence to support the notion that you are fat because you were born that way. Both the set-point theory and the fat-cell theory suggest a predisposition to weight gain above ideal body weight. *A predisposition is a tendency, a susceptibility. It is not a fait accompli.*

The set-point theory suggests a biologically programmed body weight, influenced by both genetic and environmental factors. According to this theory, if your set point is higher than your ideal weight, you will eat enough food to reach your set point, but will not gain weight above it unless you make a concerted effort to do so. As Hodgson and Miller point out, there is no conclusive evidence that the set point even exists, nor are there means to measure it. At best, this theory tells us that some of us are more susceptible to weight gain than others.

The fat-cell theory, on the other hand, suggests that some of us have a greater number of fat cells than others, and that their number is genetically determined but can also be influenced by eating patterns. The body can add fat cells during two key periods: infancy and adolescence. Again, the scientific evidence suggests a *propensity* to weight gain, not a certainty.

I like to think of the small amount of loose skin around my abdomen as the place where most of my now-flat, empty fat cells hang around screaming to be filled up again. I visualize them living there not to torment me, but rather to serve as constant reminders of my victory over their insidious demands. Slightly overweight people will "pinch an inch" and feel full fat cells. I feel my flat ones. The point is, I may have many more fat cells than skinny people do, but it's my choice whether to fill them up again or keep them lean and mean.

Metabolism: Chemical Process for Survival

Everyone has a basal metabolism, the chemical process of burning the number of calories required to keep the body alive at rest. For most adults, 1200 to 1800 calories do the job. When the body is active in movement, say in walking around the house, running in the Boston Marathon, or making love, more energy is required to sustain life.

Body weight is maintained when the energy equation is in balance. On one side of this equation are the calories you've consumed. On the other side are both the energy required for your basal metabolism and the energy for your physical activities. When you take in more calories than you burn, over a period of time, those leftover, unburned calories are stored in your body as fat.

You cannot change your basal metabolism. You can, however, change the out-of-balance energy equation, and not just by increasing your level of physical activity.

Let's look at the efficiency factor, or "thermic effect" on metabolic rate—how efficient or effective our food furnaces are. *Self-Watching* reports a study in which one to two hours after eating, the metabolic rate for thin people increased by as much as 25 percent, indicating very efficient calorie-burning furnaces. For overweight people, the increase was only 9 percent. This means we have sluggish, less efficient metabolisms. We can change the efficiency of our metabolisms, however, by becoming thin and *staying thin*. Staying thin is the key. Cyclical dieting, according to Hodgson and Miller, is what makes our metabolisms sluggish to begin with.

Other factors influencing metabolic rate cannot be changed or reversed. People who are taller and have larger bone structures have higher metabolisms. Age is another factor: older people are generally less active than younger people. And finally, women have it tougher than men; women have lower basal metabolisms. That's why, when you look at body-weight charts, you see divisions not only for age and height but for gender as well. If you are a short, forty-five-year-old woman, you do not want to eat like a twenty-year-old, six-foot man.

You cannot alter a genetic predisposition for weight gain, but you can create a food environment in which you are less susceptible to making that predisposition into a permanent fat-body disposition. You cannot alter your basal metabolism, but you can increase the efficiency and effectiveness of its thermic effect.

Remember, your genes do not make you fat; your desire to overeat and the food habits you developed to support that desire do. The thinning perspective that you have already begun to develop will help you change these two fat food realities into permanent thin ones.

CHAPTER FOUR

Basic Measurement Tools

I USED TO HATE NUMBERS. They are so exact—so black-and-white and definite. Numbers don't lie, and they aren't open to interpretation. They're just *there*, cold and unfeeling, like the bathroom scale, whose little window rolls numbers the way a slot machine rolls little figures of fruit. Only instead of spewing out cash, the scale always slides silently home to the truth. My Fat Self hated the bathroom scale. That's why I didn't own one.

But now that I was going to lose weight once and for all, I wanted to know the numbers. I used to measure the increase or decrease of my body size by how my clothes fit me. Obviously, that was not as accurate a measurement as the bathroom scale provided.

Accuracy now became important to me because it was a kind of measurement my Fat Self had always avoided, and upon which my Thin Self could grow. I still didn't like numbers, but I declared a truce with them, and I bought a bathroom scale.

Of course, I still had to learn how to use it effectively: When should I weigh myself to get maximum satisfaction out of my progress? How would I learn to use the numbers I recorded on my Weigh-In Chart, the applause of progress as well as the whispers of problems up ahead?

Some people like to weigh themselves first thing in the morning. They like being well informed regardless of whether the news is good or bad. Others make their scale part of their daily horoscope: Is this a good day or a bad one? Then there is the matter-of-fact, routine, once-a-week weigh-in.

There is also the matter of temperament. There are the shy, cautious types, like me, who initially approach their scales with trepidation and fear. Some days we are bold, with the courage of lions; on other days, we are lambs awaiting slaughter. In time, I learned to weigh in for accuracy, not judgment.

My weighing-in routine became one of practical necessity allied with my temperament. How frequently I weighed in depended on these factors: steady weight loss, plateaus, change in menu selection, menstrual cycle, high salt intake, and sometimes whether the sun was shining. I did, however, always weigh myself at the same time of day and wearing as few clothes as possible.

My little food scale, on the other hand, didn't care about my temperament. It brooked no nonsense from me. And I, in turn, was encouraged to brook no nonsense from my Fat Self. I had not bothered to weigh food portions on previous diets. I had also never succeeded on previous diets.

I knew that I would be eating 800 calories a day. For dieting purposes, calories are counted by portion sizes in ounces and grams. That meant weighing everything I ate, for one reason and one reason only: accuracy. If I ate 800 calories a day for six months, according to my doctor, I could lose 100 pounds. It was all in the numbers.

I gathered these scales and other basic measurement tools and learned how to use them because they, along with written records and observation exercises, did not lie.

My Fat Self, on the other hand, was a better prevaricator and deviator from the truth than the devil himself. Prediet, whenever I got on a friend's scale, my Fat Self would try to virtually move the number shown right before my eyes, or discredit the experience, or both: "This scale must be wrong. The shoes weigh at least two pounds each, and my clothes an additional four to five pounds."

You will begin gathering and using your basic measurement tools for the same reason I did: they will not lie to you. On the contrary, they will help keep you honest, and self-honesty is the hallmark of your thinning perspective.

You might be thinking, "But I've done all this before. I've weighed myself, my food, measured the inches around my waist and thighs, and crammed my head full of information on nutrition. All I got for my efforts was more weight." I say back to you, "Where was your Fat Self when you did all this?"

Check off the basic measurement tools that you already have from the following list. Acquire the others during your preparation time. Be sure to take along your Fat Self when you go shopping. Listen to and observe it. Your Fat Self is your best teacher of what *not* to do. When it tells you to go home empty-handed, ignore it.

Basic Measurement Tools

For measuring your body during physical changes:

1. body-weight scale (in a color of your choice)

2. full-length mirror

3. cloth tape measure

For measuring food for your Thin Self:

4. food scale (showing ounces and grams)

5. calorie counter (that lists the calorie, carbohydrate, protein, and fat contents of foods and beverages)

For recording measurements and identification of food and food habits and their changing effects on your body:

6. small spiral notebook for use as a food log

7. large spiral notebook (with dividers) for record keeping, food-habit-observation exercises, and personal
food suggestions and menu planning

To increase your personal knowledge about food and the more
healthful role it can play in your living thin:

8. a good book about nutrition (I recommend *Jane Brody's
Nutrition Book*, published by Bantam Books)

How to Use Your Measurement Tools

I kept a Weigh-In Chart beside my bathroom scale. This
chart was an indicator of the time it took to reach my weight
goal as well as a record of the consistency with which I
weighed in. Initially, because I was so heavy, I saw my Thin
Self more in terms of numbers than in real flesh. Also, just the
practice of weighing myself on a regular basis became a lesson
in establishing a new habit.

Weighing in, especially during the early part of my program, was an excellent opportunity for instruction. My Thin
Self realized that I needed *time, consistency,* and *practice* to
form new habits. My Fat Self, of course, disparaged my efforts
to establish these new habits. Weighing in was always a victory for one desire, a defeat for the other. My Fat Self, always
the sore loser, plotted schemes to discredit the obvious truth of
the numbers.

Like ritualized incantations, my Fat Self whispered as I
approached the scale, "Don't do it. You'll be sorry. Today is not
a good day. Come back tomorrow. You do not have to do this,
you know." Such incantations were part of the "how" of my Fat
Self's resistance to change. Recognition of this kind of internal
verbal warfare was essential in applying countertactics to accomplish change on behalf of my Thin Self.

Following is a twelve-month summary of my Weigh-In
Chart. It shows how I used a basic measurement tool to answer

Twelve-Month Summary of My Weight Loss

	Date	Body Weight	Pounds Lost
FIRST MONTH	Sept 1, 1981 Sept 30	240 220	20
SECOND MONTH	Oct 1 Oct 31	220 207	13
THIRD MONTH	Nov 1 Nov 30	207 198	9
FOURTH MONTH	Dec 1 Dec 31	198 189	9
FIFTH MONTH	Jan 1, 1982 Jan 31	189 180	9
SIXTH MONTH	Feb 1 Feb 28	180 174	6
SEVENTH MONTH	Mar 1 Mar 31	174 152	22
EIGHTH MONTH	Apr 1 Apr 30	152 146	6
NINTH MONTH	May 1 May 31	146 142	4
TENTH MONTH	June 1 June 30	142 134	8
ELEVENTH MONTH	July 1 July 31	134 126	8
TWELFTH MONTH	Aug 1 Aug 31	126 120	6

1983 Metropolitan Height and Weight Tables for Men and Women

According to Frame, Ages 25–59

HEIGHT (IN SHOES)†		SMALL FRAME	MEDIUM FRAME	LARGE FRAME
		Weight in Pounds (In Indoor Clothing)*		
		MEN		
Feet	**Inches**			
5	2	128–134	131–141	138–150
5	3	130–136	133–143	140–153
5	4	132–138	135–145	142–156
5	5	134–140	137–148	144–160
5	6	136–142	139–151	146–164
5	7	138–145	142–154	149–168
5	8	140–148	145–157	152–172
5	9	142–151	148–160	155–176
5	10	144–154	151–163	158–180
5	11	146–157	154–166	161–184
6	0	149–160	157–170	164–188
6	1	152–164	160–174	168–192
6	2	155–168	164–178	172–197
6	3	158–172	167–182	176–202
6	4	162–176	171–187	181–207
		WOMEN		
4	10	102–111	109–121	118–131
4	11	103–113	111–123	120–134
5	0	104–115	113–126	122–137
5	1	106–118	115–129	125–140
5	2	108–121	118–132	128–143
5	3	111–124	121–135	131–147
5	4	114–127	124–138	134–151
5	5	117–130	127–141	137–155
5	6	120–133	130–144	140–159
5	7	123–136	133–147	143–163
5	8	126–139	136–150	146–167
5	9	129–142	139–153	149–170
5	10	132–145	142–156	152–173
5	11	135–148	145–159	155–176
6	0	138–151	148-162	158–179

*Indoor clothing weighing 5 pounds for men and 3 pounds for women.
Courtesy of the Metropolitan Life Insurance Company
†Shoes with 1-inch heels.
Source of basic data: *Build Study, 1979*, Society of Actuaries and Association of Life Insurance Medical Directors of America, 1980.
Copyright 1983 Metropolitan Life Insurance Company.

such "whispered" attempts to undermine my decision to live thin. My body-weight scale and Weigh-In Chart were two of the resoundingly successful "hows" of my accomplishment.

To set up your Weigh-In Chart, you must first determine your ideal weight range. Use the accompanying height-and-weight tables to guide you in determining your ideal weight range if your doctor has not provided it for you. The numbers on the tables are not written in stone. Your best source for accuracy is your doctor, who knows you personally, your age, and especially your dieting history. These factors must be taken into account to identify your *realistic* ideal weight range.

Now, take out your large notebook, and in the section you mark "Record Keeping" copy out the following Personal Weekly Weigh-In Chart. Enter your realistic weight range goal in the appropriate space. Your weekly chart is now ready to be filled in daily, twice a week, or once a week.

Personal Weekly Weigh-In Chart

Program Goal: My Ideal Weight Range _____

	Sun	Mon	Tues	Wed	Thur	Fri	Sat	Pounds Lost
FIRST WEEK								
SECOND WEEK								
THIRD WEEK								
FOURTH WEEK								

You may also want to keep a monthly summary of your Weekly Weigh-In Chart, as I did; use the Record Keeping section for this purpose. If you are losing 30 pounds or more, I recommend keeping this second weight chart. Recording your weight figures a second time may seem boring and tedious, like balancing your checkbook. But make no mistake about it; you learn to manage real body weight with real numbers. Every time you record these numbers you are taking back control of your weight.

Set up your monthly summary chart to look like the one below. Fill it out at the end of each month.

Monthly Summary Weight Chart

	Actual Date	Body Weight	Pounds Lost
FIRST MONTH			
SECOND MONTH			
THIRD MONTH			

Keep in mind these recommendations as you prepare to weigh in and record your progress toward your goal.

- Keep your Weekly Weigh-In Chart near your scale. Post it on the wall or attach it to a clipboard to be kept in a drawer.
- Weigh yourself consistently throughout your three-phase personal food-plan diet. Whether you weigh in once a day, once a week, or several times a week, be consistent. There will be some weeks when you want to weigh yourself daily, other weeks less frequently. Be guided by your temperament at such times, but do pick at least one specific day each week to weigh in. Also, be sure always to weigh in at the same time of day and with

48

the same weight of clothes. Your Fat Self will try to steer you away from consistent weigh-ins. Acknowledge such instructions of avoidance but *do not follow them.* Instead, follow your Thin Self's consistent plan to weigh in. With practice, that consistency will become a new habit to strengthen your Thin Self.

- If you hit a plateau and stop losing weight temporarily, do not panic and dump your personal diet. Your Fat Self will urge you to be impatient—one of the attributes of the diet mentality. Grit your teeth, take a deep breath, and say out loud one of the words your Fat Self truly hates: "*patience.*" Then practice it.

Full-Length Mirror

I never cared for mirrors, especially the full-length variety, and I usually avoided them like the plague. What I saw in them was a fat woman staring back at me.

When Dr. Wilson suggested I buy a full-length mirror, I did so reluctantly. I brought it home, hung it on my bedroom door, and promptly walked away. I'd give it a good workout, I told myself when I was safely in another room, after I began losing weight.

I caught the presence of this avoidance attitude immediately. What was I trying to avoid—seeing my Fat Self and confirming visually the power and consequences of my fat food habits? Then I realized that if I allowed my Fat Self to prevent me from looking at it, it had even more power over me than I had thought. It was a frightening thought.

I looked in the mirror.

I genuinely wanted to have pity and compassion for what I saw: not the 240 pounds of flesh, but rather the gamut of feelings reflected in my eyes. I saw pain and sadness and flickers of despair. Then, *boom!*—darts of rebellion and anger, conceit and deceitfulness. If I hadn't been so heavy already, I think the visual proof of my desire to be fat might have knocked me over.

49

That, I discovered, was the essential purpose of my full-length mirror—*to help me to become consciously aware of both of my desires.* If I was going to change my Fat Self, to replace the desire to overeat with my desire to be slim, I needed to be consciously aware of both desires, in order to actively *and honestly* make the right choice between them.

"But what," you might ask, "would happen if I went to my full-length mirror, stared at my overweight body, and became so overwhelmed by the truth and just how much I have to lose that I got too depressed to go on?"

My answer is this: Confront your visual image armed with resolve in your heart and the words *Choice* and *It's my own decision to live thin.* Either write them down and tape them on the mirror, or be prepared to utter them repeatedly, loudly if need be. Give your Thin Self its own verbal incantation to affirm your goal and to begin countering the "Don't do it. You'll be sorry" incantations of your Fat Self.

As you prepare to stand before your mirror, keep in mind the following:

- Your body is the visible proof of your desire to overeat. Actually seeing its reflection is your opportunity to acknowledge that desire.
- Rather than focusing on feelings of guilt and shame over your desire to overeat, allow yourself to feel the courage, the hope, and the self-honesty you now bring to your body shape through your thinning perspective and in the form of your desire to slim down permanently.
- Allow yourself to feel the presence of this other desire every time you stand before your full-length mirror. Congratulate yourself for having consciously chosen to welcome it and to pursue its attainment.

Cloth Tape Measure

Like your body-weight scale, this tool becomes a measure of the progress of your Thin Self when you record monthly readings on your Inch-by-Inch Body Measurement Chart.

If remembered feelings of previously kept charts pop into your head and urge your resistance to doing so again, ask yourself where the resistance is coming from. Listen for your Fat Self's avoidance attitude.

Take your physical measurements during your preparation time, before you begin losing weight, preferably in front of your full-length mirror. Touching as well as seeing your overweight body before and during its physical changes can increase and complement your awareness of your Thin Self as it emerges from the inside out as your body thins from the outside in.

Set up your Inch-by-Inch Body Measurement Chart in the Record Keeping section of your large notebook as follows.

Inch-by-Inch Body Measurement Chart

DATE	WEIGHT	CLOTH-ING SIZE	Neck (for men)	Upper Arm	Chest	Waist	Hips	Upper Thighs	Calves
___	___	___							
___	___	___							
___	___	___							
___	___	___							

I recommend taking your measurements each time you lose ten pounds or more. A ten-pound loss is usually followed by a change in clothing size.

As you prepare to record your physical changes inch-by-inch, keep in mind the following:

• The heavier you are, the larger your measurements will be. As you reduce your body weight, you will also reduce the number of inches. Acknowledge this thinning perspective, daily if need be.

- Regardless of how many pounds you must lose to reach your weight goal, do not let your Fat Self overwhelm you with remembrances of the yo-yo syndrome and accompanying feelings of failure. Acknowledge such admonishments. Do not follow your Fat Self's advice to quit the program while you are still ahead.

- For most women, fatty-tissue storage is more plentiful in the lower abdomen and upper thighs. When you gain weight, the inches are often added here first. When you reverse the weight gain and begin to lose, these inches generally come off last. Most of the fatty tissue does come off, in time. However, do not expect to look like either Twiggy or Raquel Welch.

- When you read fashion books that describe body measurements corresponding to clothing sizes, you are walking the edge of a fantasy pit of unrealistic expectations into which your Fat Self would like to push you. Do not be tempted by the injunction that your numbers must match those of professional models, who are paid to approximate perfections the vast majority of human bodies do not reflect. Many women, myself included, wear one size in blouses and jackets and a different size in skirts and slacks.

Calorie Counter and Nutrition Book

For me, learning about food was like walking into a highschool English class: I thought I already knew everything. However, I quickly discovered how wrong I was.

Here I was, thirty-six years old, and I did not know that one gram of protein contains the same number of calories (4) as one gram of carbohydrate, or that fat contains 9 calories per gram. No wonder I always gained weight when I ate bread: I didn't butter my bread, I breaded my butter. And I used to eat the rims of fat around steaks with as much gusto as I ate the meat itself. I always ate large portions of meat that were heavily marbled with fat, for the taste and tenderness of the protein. I had to keep my strength up. Even I knew (or thought I did) how important lots of protein, preferably in the form of fatty red beef, was for keeping one strong and healthy. Instead, it kept me fat and increasingly unhealthy.

The more I read my little *Food and Drink Counter*, the more misinformed I felt. I began to berate myself for my poor eating habits, my lack of nutritional knowledge, and for believing the television commercials that told me: "Try it, you'll like it." "It's good for you." "I ate the whole thing."

Then I realized that the important thing right now, during my preparation time, was to figure out what I could eat that made up 800 calories per day and had maximum nutritional value.

Leafing through my calorie counter when I first bought it, I knew that I wasn't going to learn the basic nutrition and calorie contents of everything under the sun and in my refrigerator in one day. I had not gained my excess weight in one day. I was not going to take it off in one day, either.

This is why diet-preparation time is so crucial to the success of your personally designed program. While your Fat Self is busy instructing you in overweight maintenance, you, the designer, are actively teaching yourself patience, which is an attribute of your thinning perspective.

Take time now to read *Jane Brody's Nutrition Book*. Learning about nutrition before you begin losing weight will help you to get thin, and it is essential for staying thin.

Food Log and Food Scale

The food log and food scale are familiar measuring tools to many cyclical dieters. But I had never used either one before I designed my own program: I had never had the patience to write it all down or to weigh it all out. My adamant avoidance attitude, signaling the presence of my Fat Self, had been stronger than my desire to overcome it.

I overcame that attitude with consistent practice in using both the food scale and the food log. For each morsel of food I put into my mouth, I weighed it out first and recorded it afterward. As I did so, I reminded myself that what I weighed out and recorded were not "diet foods for an overweight body." Rather, they were simply foods for a thin person. This awareness became part of my thinning perspective. However, the change did not occur overnight. I had nineteen years of a diet-mentality attitude toward food to overcome.

My food-log entries of fish, poultry, meat, milk products, fresh fruits, vegetables, and whole grains and cereals were not diet foods. They were foods everyone ate, with all the variety and richness of taste and texture that thin people have been enjoying for years. (Absent, of course, were the frequently eaten high-calorie foods for overweight maintenance.)

Consistently weighing and recording these common, ordinary foods, every time I ate, were two of the first thin food habits I developed. Every time I used these tools, I was living as a thin person.

Your small notebook is your Food Log for a Thin Person. Set up each page to record the following:

- date
- all food and caloric beverages consumed
- corresponding caloric value for each item listed
- total daily calorie intake

You can simply list each item and its caloric value at the time you eat it. This is quick and convenient. On the other hand, if you're always in a hurry and out of patience with food, you should begin to retrain yourself by taking the time to add additional information and set up your daily food-log entry as follows:

Meal	Calories Per Item	Total Calories
Date		**Body Weight Today**
BREAKFAST item, portion size, how prepared		
LUNCH		
AFTERNOON SNACK		
DINNER		
EVENING SNACK		
Day's Total		

55

Keep in mind the following as you prepare to weigh and record food for your Thin Self:

- Numbers on a scale and in written records do not lie, nor are they subject to a memory infiltrated and distorted by your Fat Self, who, prediet, might have piped up, "If you can't remember exactly what you ate yesterday, don't worry, you can make up for it today."
- In order to count the calories in the foods and beverages you consume, you must learn their calorie contents. Consistent daily practice in recording caloric values will help you to memorize them.
- Record *all* foods and beverages consumed each day. Teaspoons, tablespoons, handfuls, and quarter-cup measurements count. Do not consume calories without first counting them. This kind of awareness will strengthen your Thin Self and help restore *your* control over food.
- Record actual caloric values. Do not round them off to the nearest low whole number. For example, 4 ounces of fresh cod has 88 calories, not 80; 4 ounces of broiled chicken, without skin, has 155 calories, not 150; 1 ounce of cheddar cheese has 106 calories, not 100. Your Fat Self disparages accuracy as well as the thinning-perspective attributes of patience and being realistic.
- Be honest. You do not have to lie, cheat, or deviate from the truth. Your Fat Self has done enough of that already.
- Remember for whom you are painstakingly weighing and recording all these foods and beverages. Be supportive of your hard work with hand painted signs magnetized to your refrigerator: "Foods for My Thin Self." Tape a typed message to your food scale: "Foods for My Thin Self Weighed Here Daily."
- Finally, your food log is a recorded remembrance of success. Over time, both during your program as well as following it, this record helps replace memories of past failures.

56

Habit-Observation Exercises

Habit-observation exercises are an integral part of your personal diet program. Before you can begin changing your food habits, you must first identify them clearly. I believe the best way to do this is in writing. If you write it down, you will not forget it. Remember, memory failure is a Fat Self tactic to keep you overweight. By writing down your observations of your eating patterns, you will increase your awareness of your Fat Self's destructive habits and binge triggers, which are your "secret" attitudes and feelings about food.

For those of you who have kept behavior diaries while following other diet programs, remember that you will be doing things differently this time. The purpose of keeping a behavior diary is to observe your food habits and the environmental influences that trigger them into action.

Begin these exercises now, during your preparation time. Take time to do them calmly, deliberately, and with patience. Do not expect to complete them in one sitting. You did not develop your food habits in one day: you will not become consciously aware of all of them in one day either. Work on these exercises throughout your program, preferably during a quiet time you set aside for yourself each day.

I do not recommend writing down your observations immediately after eating. If you try to watch your desire to overeat too closely, your Fat Self might decide to put on a bow tie and behave itself, then sneak up on you with its nasty habits and sabotage your diet later, when you least expect it.

In the Habit-Observation section (marked on the divider) of your large notebook, make three separate food-habit lists based on your observations and your Fat Self's instructions for overweight maintenance. Allow for some information overlap, as the areas to be covered are: everyday eating habits; selection and preparation habits; and binge triggers.

Since your Fat Self will be your teacher in these exercises, it's helpful to acknowledge its presence and invite its active participation in identifying specific instructions for over-weight maintenance. If you're having trouble finding the voice of this desire, just think "food."

After each observation-and-recording session, reward your hard work with a cup of hot tea, a quiet relaxing bath, or some other activity that makes you feel good about yourself. Remember, food is not a reward. Eating would only make your Fat Self feel good, and that is exactly what we're trying to avoid.

Everyday Eating Habits

To help you begin to identify the first set of food habits—how you eat and drink your calories—write down your an-swers to the following questions. Do not hesitate to add questions that pertain to your lifestyle.

- How fast do you eat? Is your plate empty while everyone else's is still full? Do you eat a complete meal during TV commercials or during the course of a half-hour TV pro-gram?
- Do you always use big plates, even for snacks?
- How much food do you put on your fork and how many bites does it take you to eat an apple, a sandwich, or a chicken leg?
- Do you gulp your beverages or sip them?
- Do you cut your food into bite-size pieces or fat-size pieces?
- Do you eat while doing something else, like watching TV, reading, or walking or driving back to work after lunch?
- How often do you eat? Are you a daytime snacker, an hourly nibbler, or a midnight refrigerator raider? Do you skip meals, then make up for it at the next one?
- Do you anticipate the pleasure of eating your next meal while finishing the current one? Do you think about eating all the time, most of the time, or just some of the time?

List of Selection and Preparation Habits

Once you have begun to recognize your eating habits, you can begin to look more closely at the habits you've developed in selecting and preparing the foods you eat. It is likely that you practice these selection and preparation habits with very little conscious awareness, because you probably inherited most of them from your parents. You did not question, as a child, how food was gathered and taste enhanced; you ate what was put in front of you. To begin identifying this set of food habits, you must now begin questioning them.

In completing this second observation exercise, do not answer just *yes* or *no* to the following questions. Write out the actual habit you practice. Again, add questions that pertain to your own lifestyle.

- Do you shop for food at a regularly scheduled time or usually at the urging of your desire to indulge?
- Do you go to the big supermarket where all the high calories are stored under one roof, or do you specialty shop in a number of stores for choice selections in meat, fish, produce, etc.?
- Do you "leave the shopping to someone else" and passively eat whatever is put in front of you?
- If someone else does the food shopping, do you have a say in what is selected for your overweight body?
- Do you take the time to plan meals, or do you simply select, prepare, and cook whatever is most convenient?
- Do you spend more time eating food than in gathering it?
- Do you always select the same basic food staples, then prepare and cook them the same way?
- Do you always mash potatoes, bread and fry fish or chicken, or use lots of butter and/or sugar to enhance the taste of other foods?
- How much butter, oil, sugar, and salt do you use on a weekly basis in preparing your food?

- Do you avoid foods that are not prepared with taste enhancers such as oils and sugars, believing that such "plain" foods are too bland?
- Do you believe that foods prepared with sugar or butter taste better than others, rather than just different from them?
- Do you read recipe books looking for variety and diversity in selecting and preparing basic food staples?
- If you do not know how to cook, are you willing to learn?
- If you do not know how to enhance the taste of foods without using lots of oils and refined sugars or honey, are you willing to learn?
- If you are a milk drinker but do not like the taste of low- or nonfat milk and related products, are you willing to acquire a taste for them?

Your answers to the last three questions in particular are directly tied to your Fat Self desire, which maintains your overweight body. If you are not willing to change the food habits that feed your Fat Self, you will not learn how to live thin.

Listen for the diet-mentality attitude behind your answers. If you are at least *willing*, during this preparation time, *to consider new food-gathering and tasting techniques*, that willingness is a clear indication of your newly developing thinning perspective.

Binge Triggers

Binge triggers are the toughest food habits to identify and write down because they are so closely associated with our feelings and thoughts about ourselves. Binge triggers involve how we see ourselves acting and reacting in a sometimes unfriendly world of thin people, many of whom don't think very highly of us because we don't look like them.

60

Binge triggers can be anything at all—a person, a thought, a place, a single feeling like depression or anger or anxiety, or a simple statement like "I love you" or "Why don't you lose weight?" They can be other people's suggestions of "Try it, you'll like it," or "One more won't make much difference." A binge trigger can also be a single favorite food.

Binge triggers are excuses and rationalizations for removing self-restraint, common sense, and conscious awareness of your eating habits. They set off eating sprees you feel powerless to stop until you are either sated or physically sick. I've come to think of my binge triggers as surprise announcements of one-act powerplays in which my Fat Self stars.

Do not expect to complete this exercise of identifying your triggers in one sitting. As with the two preceding exercises, you will want to work on it throughout your program. The purpose of observing and recording your food habits is to learn exactly what they are and what lies behind them. You cannot change your food habits without thorough knowledge of both.

Keep in mind the following as you begin to observe and record your binge triggers:

- Ask yourself not *why* but rather *how* these sprees happen. What specifically sets them off for you?
- Search your memory for previous binges that were triggered by specific, recurring thoughts and feelings.
- Look particularly for feelings of sadness, anxiousness, and self-pity that have, in the past, consistently and cunningly soothed your heart and mind through your stomach. Are there patterns of specific people, places, and experiences that set those feelings and thoughts in motion? If so, what are the patterns?
- Ask your Fat Self if there are certain foods you cannot eat just a little of and from which you cannot easily walk away.
- Look for various activities that consistently trigger eat-

ing sprees, like dancing or other vigorous physical activity, drinking with friends after work, or attending entertainment or sports events.

Putting Your Fat Self Food Knowledge to Thinning Use

Once you have started identifying your fat food habits, begin to compare them with food habits that do not make you fat. Remember, use your personal diet tools not only to make you consciously aware of your internal desire to overeat, but to encourage, support, and reward your desire to live thin.

Everyone has food habits. Overweight individuals, however, develop special food habits that make and keep them fat. These habits include a preference for high-calorie foods, excessive quantities, increased frequency of eating, and primarily negative-based thoughts and feelings infiltrating the relationship between the overweight individual and food.

Let's look at some common food habits practiced by many thin people and the ways in which our habits differ from theirs.

Food Habits

Typical Food Habit	Fat Response	Thin Response
food preference	candy bar snack	fresh fruit snack
quantity of eating	second helping	one average portion
frequency of eating	four or more daily meals	two–three daily meals
feelings and food	eating because of unpleasant feelings	not eating when emotionally upset
thoughts and food	eating during social occasions	socializing during social occasions

To help turn the habit-observation exercises you've been doing here into basic tools to help your thin desire, make up your own chart. Again, do not expect to complete this exercise in one sitting. Begin now. Add to it more features as you progress through your program. It is not only a tool for increasing your food-habit awareness; it shows you, in black-and-white, which foods and habits will keep you overweight and which will help you to live thin. It also strengthens your thinning perspective, as it serves as a constant reminder that you *do have a clear choice*—something your Fat Self would like to rob you of.

To set up your chart, first list the fat responses you practice, then fill in the opposite, thin responses. Last, list the typical food habits to which they apply. For example, if you are a speed eater, leave the shopping to others, use lots of butter and oils in cooking, fry chicken and fish, eat to ward off boredom, and nibble your way through an anxiety-filled day, this is what your chart would look like.

Typical Food Habit	Fat Response	Thin Response
eating time	speed eater	eat slowly
food selection	have no say in food selection	help select healthful foods
enhancing food taste	lots of butter and oils	moderate use of butter and oils
cooking method	fry chicken and fish	broil or steam
thoughts and food	eat to ward off boredom	noneating activity to rouse interest
feelings and food	constant nibbling to assuage anxiety	noneating activity to release anxiety

63

All of the tools discussed in this chapter will help you to become consciously aware of both of your food desires. With self-awareness, you can make a conscious choice between which desire you want to act upon. Every time you choose your thin desire you are strengthening your thinning perspective and learning to live thin *before* you lose the first fat pound. This, in turn, will give you added fortification against your Fat Self's resistance to change when you actually begin to alter your eating habits.

You must now prepare yourself to meet that resistance to change, which is sure to come.

CHAPTER FIVE

Personal Diet Tactics

THE REAL STRUGGLE IN DIETING does not take place at midnight as you stand in front of your refrigerator, or when you are eating at home or in a restaurant, or even while you're passing your favorite bakery. For many of you, these will be scenes of confrontation, but the real struggle over food and its role in your life will take place inside you. Your Fat Self is going to resist your decision to live thin.

You have already begun preparing for success, by developing a thinning perspective and learning how to use personal diet tools. Now it's time to begin to change your Fat Self desire, by learning how to use personal diet tactics.

Personal diet tactics are conscious, deliberate practices to help you to change your Fat Self's resistance to change and to permanently replace your fat food desire with a thin food desire. These tactics depend not on willpower, but on your capacity to be honest with yourself in consciously choosing to continue to live fat or instead to live thin. Self-honesty is the key ingredient of your personal diet program. It is your personal guide to permanent weight loss and to overcoming your resistance to this goal.

Personal diet tactics are based on certain truths about dieting that all overweighters find difficult to accept. These fundamental truths about how we see ourselves in relation to food

65

are an essential part of our thinning perspective. They set the stage for overcoming our Fat Self's resistance to change.

Your Fat Self cannot hear, much less accept, these truths. But you, the director of your personal diet program, can hear them. And you must choose consciously to listen and to accept them during your preparation time.

These truths are as follows:

- The purpose of dieting is to learn how to maintain a realistic thin weight once it's achieved. The purpose is not to inflict on you a constant state of deprivation of one of life's basic necessities—food—or of a basic sensory pleasure—eating.
- Permanent weight loss is usually accomplished by learning to control daily calorie intake and to replace fat-adding food habits with thin ones, ultimately making these your normal food habits. Weight loss cannot be sustained if you continue to eat whatever you want whenever you want it; you cannot live thin and eat like an overweight person.
- Dieting cannot be successful when your attitude is one of haste and impatience. Your excess weight was not gained in one day; it will not come off and stay off in one day.

Do not expect to fully accept these truths about dieting in one day. Right now your attentions are focused on losing weight and losing it as quickly as possible. But, since you also want to keep that weight off, you must focus also on these truths.

These truths tell you where the resistance of your Fat Self is. In order to win this struggle, you must learn to recognize the characteristics of this resistance, because out of these will come your personal diet tactics. In fact, your personal diet tactics are the reverse of your Fat Self's resistance tactics.

Following are the chief characteristics of your Fat Self's resistance tactics. Memorize them.

- *Self-Negation.* Avoidance and denial are the ways in which your Fat Self says "no" to your desire for thinness. For example, when you look in your mirror or at the numbers on a body-weight scale or the items recorded in your food log, all of which remind you of your choice for thinness, your Fat Self tries to negate what your eyes see, and also negates the fact that you do have a choice in what you eat, how you look to yourself and others, and how you feel about yourself and food.

- *Self-Indulgence.* Out-of-control, indulgent food experiences are another way in which your Fat Self urges you to eat whatever you want whenever you want it. Such experiences are your Fat Self's way of saying "yes" to itself regardless of the consequences to your physical and emotional well-being. For example, when you are physically and/or emotionally exhausted and plan to head for a hot, soothing bath, or quiet time in your favorite chair with your pet or listening to music, all of which are healthy releases for you and your body, your Fat Self demands hysterically or whispers subtly in your ear, "Eat, you'll feel better."

- *Impatience.* Your Fat Self likes to do everything that relates to food as though there is no tomorrow. It may prompt you to eat every meal as the last meal, or to hurry through this program so that you can get back to "normal." For example, while your attentions are focused on losing weight, there is that thought at the back of your mind urging you to do it fast. Regardless of how quickly you lose weight, it never seems fast enough.

Following are the chief characteristics of your personal diet tactics, which are the reverse of your Fat Self's resistance characteristics. Memorize these, too.

- *Self-Affirmation.* Actively say "yes" to your decision to live thin, especially in response to your Fat Self's attempts to negate that decision and negate *you* in the process.

- *Self-Discipline*. Actively say "no" to your desire to over-eat with the same firm tone of voice a parent uses to prevent an out-of-control child from doing something harmful to himself.
- *Patience*. Actively make time your ally rather than your enemy. It is not you who is running out of time learning how to live thin: it is your Fat Self keeping you over-weight.

For me, turning the above characteristics into specific personal diet tactics involved two things: first, observing my Fat Self's instructions for keeping me overweight after I made the decision to live thin; and then consciously reversing these resistance instructions.

Following are some of the personal diet tactics I used to reverse my Fat Self's instructions to keep me overweight. I often practiced several tactics simultaneously when I met especially heavy resistance in this struggle.

The "Yes" Tactic

On previous diets, I had always said "no" to my Fat Self. This time, instead of focusing on the negative, I needed to say "yes" to my Thin Self, not only to relieve the sinking feeling of constant denial, but to strengthen my thinning perspective.

I began by saying "yes" in coming to a decision to live thin, and I continued to do so during preparation and my personal food-plan diet:

- Yes, I will look in my full-length mirror.
- Yes, this plate of food for a thin person does look lovely.
- Yes, cooking with wine or lemon and herbs will be different from cooking with lots of butter and salt. One kind of taste is not necessarily better than the other: they are merely different from each other, and so are their calorie contents.

- Yes, I do believe a piece of fresh fruit for dessert will satisfy my sweet tooth.
- Yes, I'm so hungry I could eat a horse. But I'll munch on fresh raw vegetables, which have far fewer calories than a cooked horse.
- Yes, I am feeling anxious. I will feel much better, and so will my tense body, if I relax in a hot bath.

The "No" Tactic

Of course, there were times when I had to say "no" to my desire to overeat. But saying "no" on my personal diet program did not present a problem. Nor did exercising good old-fashioned discipline over my overweight food habits make me feel like I could not do what I wanted. On the contrary, I practiced this "no" tactic in order to accomplish what I did want, which was to live thin for the rest of my life.

- No, my bathroom scale is not broken because the numbers are too high. I'm going to bring those numbers down, not throw out this scale.
- No, I'm not going to write my food-log entries in pencil so that I can erase them.
- No, I'm not going to put ice cream and chocolate syrup on top of my fresh fruit slices to satisfy my sweet tooth.
- No, I'm not going to go to that particular restaurant, because the menu does not include lean-cuisine entrees and the high-calorie entree portions are too large.
- No, I'm not going to eat so fast that I forget what I'm eating or the fact that I am eating.

The Time Tactic

For as long as I can remember, I was a meal skipper, a quick cooker of processed, canned and frozen foods, and a gobble-it-up, wolf-it-down, and bay-for-more speed eater. I ate so fast that by the time I finished a meal I had little recollection of even having started it.

I had certainly wanted to hurry through previous diets. "Thank goodness I only have to diet for another few days [or a week, or three]." Unwilling to use time to its fullest advantage, and not knowing how, I denied its presence, as in, "I can't take the time to do the things I know would be really good for me, like cooking healthful foods or taking a brisk walk." I ran through previous diets, ran out of time to be good to myself, and ran right into the yo-yo syndrome. Clearly, I was not the master of my life. I was a runaway victim of both time and the food in my life.

During my preparation time, I faced an enormous challenge—learning how to become the master of my food habits and my use of time. It was a Chinese proverb that ultimately helped me: "Put aside the necessary for the urgent, and abandon both for the essential."

Time became the essential tactic. Whenever I felt it slipping through my fingers while dieting, I borrowed it from other necessary activities. Often I practiced my time tactic simultaneously with other tactics. For example:

- My Fat Self would tell me I had no time for breakfast and order me to skip it and make up for it at lunch or dinner or both. I said "no" to this order and consistently adhered to regularly scheduled mealtimes. Regular scheduling was one of my time tactics.
- My Fat Self preferred canned, mashable, quickly cooked foods that could be eaten without being cut up or chewed. My new habits for selecting and preparing fresh foods that had to be cut up and chewed became time tactics to slow me down and also to say "yes" to my increasing awareness of my eating habits.

The Choice Tactic

What do you do when you find yourself feeling ravenous for something you know you shouldn't eat but feel you have no choice but to eat it? Occasionally I found my food desire out of control. However, instead of saying "no" to the desire to overeat, I said "no" to my Fat Self's food choices, and "yes" to the foods my Thin Self chose. For example, instead of indulging in a double cheeseburger, I would eat an entire head of lettuce, one leaf at a time. It was not an easy choice to make, but I succeeded.

Switching from butter to low- or no-calorie seasonings was one of the hardest choices I practiced. At first, I did not like the sour taste of fresh lemon juice and herbs or nonfat yoghurt. But I practiced this choice tactic repeatedly and consistently, and eventually my taste preference changed. This change would not have occurred had I not practiced my choice tactic. Nor would I have found the increasing range of low-calorie foods that I genuinely enjoyed.

The Attitude Tactic

Attitudes, which are learned mental positions, can sometimes be practiced with the force of written laws. My Fat Self practiced two kinds of attitudes to resist my goal to live thin. The first was a selfish attitude, as in "It's my food and you can't take it away from me." The second, equally mischievous and ultimately deadly, was an unrealistic attitude that, perhaps more than any other resistance tactic, demanded constant vigilance and near-constant practice of my reverse tactic—a realistic attitude.

For example, when I went food shopping and passed by shelves laden with high-calorie items, I sometimes felt wistful longings for the "good old days" when jams, dessert toppings, cream, sausages, doughnuts, and cookies were my standard fare. Why, my Fat Self pleaded pathetically, couldn't they be so

71

again? I practiced my realistic-attitude tactic by looking at forbidden items through my thinning perspective: they were standard foods for an overweight person, not for me, who was actively thinning from the inside out. This tactic helped me to discipline my Fat Self's unrealistic attitude toward forbidden foods and to overcome its resistance to my consistently shopping lean.

The most extreme form of my Fat Self's attitude toward food was the belief that I could have a thin body and still eat whatever I wanted whenever I wanted it—the ultimate fantasy of many overweight people. I practiced my realistic-attitude tactic almost daily throughout my program, and especially during the third phase of my diet, when I was increasing my calorie intake to halt the weight-loss process and begin maintenance. This tactic also helped me, more than any other single factor, to resist my Fat Self's proposal to become a bulimic. Had I accepted that insidious proposal, I would simply have replaced one food problem with another.

The Compromise Tactic

To me, living thin did not mean going from one extreme to another—from indulgence to abstinence. I wanted neither to glut my pleasure in eating nor to come to fear it.

I learned the compromise tactic during holiday meals with my family. On these occasions, I did not refrain from taking a taste (and I do mean one, not several) of my favorite dishes. I did not, however, exceed my daily calorie allotment. My compromise tactic not only allowed me an occasional taste treat, it helped to silence others' criticisms of my commitment to dieting.

Practicing this compromise tactic, especially at the end of my first dieting phase when Thanksgiving arrived, helped prepare me to move into Phase Two, when my menu change called for increased flexibility in food selection without increasing calories. Flexibility was at the root of my compromise tactic.

The Trick Tactic

Binge triggers, as you are learning from observing your own, are devious tricks your Fat Self pulls on you to make you eat when you are not hungry or to stuff yourself far beyond the point at which you are full.

Early in my program, my Fat Self began using binge triggers as trick tactics to prevent me from carrying out my decision to live thin. For example, prediet, junk-food commercials on TV went straight to my stomach. Producers of these commercials and my Fat Self have a lot in common. During my diet I did not stop watching television. However, when I heard the sound of that trigger going off inside me, I practiced my own trick tactic to counter it.

Whenever a commercial came on, I closed my eyes, covered my ears, conjured up a gruesome image of how I would feel if I ate the fat-laden junk food, and said out loud: "If I put one bite of that junk food into my body, when I feel it hit my stomach, I'll feel acid hit, too—an acid so strong that it will burn right through my stomach and into my intestines, leaving behind giant holes that will quickly fill with blood. The acid will continue down my legs and into my big toes, which will begin to turn black and fall off." By the time I got to my big toes, the commercial would be over.

Granted, this trick is extreme, but it effectively reversed my Fat Self's attempt to set off an eating spree after I had already eaten dinner.

My Fat Self tried other, less-extreme trick tactics, but I reversed them, too, into tricks of accomplishment. One of my Fat Self's favorite binge triggers was to give me a sudden visual image of some succulent fat food. My response was to "trick" the fat out of the food while retaining its visual appeal, and then actually prepare the defatted food for my next scheduled meal or snack.

For example, if the fat food was a big slice of apple pie, I "tricked" the fat out of it by slicing a fresh apple into quarter-inch slivers and arranging them on a fine china dessert plate with a sprinkle of cinnamon and a spring of parsley. I then brewed a pot of tea, set my table with my best linen and silverware, lit a candle, and put on my favorite music. I'd sit down feeling immeasurably pleased. I did not answer the phone, read a book, or in any other way divert my attention from what I was eating and how wonderful it was that I cared enough about myself to prepare it so beautifully.

The message behind all of my Fat Self's tactics was to get me to eat and eat and eat, especially high-calorie foods. This "eat, eat, eat" sometimes took on the sound of an incantation beating inside my head. I responded to this fat-command trick by reversing it to a thin-command trick: "a hundred pounds in six months." I took these numbers from Dr. Wilson's prediction of success when he first proposed the 800-calorie personal food-plan diet. This diet tactic took me all the way through my weight loss and into maintenance.

Gathering Your Personal Diet Tactics

The key to gathering your personal diet tactics is not to ask yourself why, when you've already made the decision to live thin, you are now experiencing resistance to it. It is not you who are resisting, it is your Fat Self. You must ask yourself how and in what specific ways you experience this resistance. When you look within and listen for instructions, your Fat Self is going to tell you how to stay overweight. Your personal diet tactics are the reverse of these instructions.

You will experience resistance during each part of your program. And it will take time for you to gather and learn to use your personal diet tactics. You can begin now, however, to gather and actually practice those personal tactics that are the reverse of your resistance. You can also practice personal tactics to help you accept the three essential truths about dieting (see p. 66) and make them part of your thinning perspective during this preparation time.

Practicing Your Personal Diet Tactics

During this preparation time, you might want to draw from the following recommendations for practicing your personal diet tactics.

- Practice the "yes" tactic on behalf of your Thin Self, not your Fat Self, which has its own resistance tactic for saying "yes" to itself, and never for your benefit. This is why you must observe and learn to distinguish between your opposing food desires. Your Fat Self may attempt to confuse you as to which desire you are saying "yes" to.

- Saying "no" is not the only tactic for controlling your desire to overeat. Other personal tactics to restore control include saying "yes" to your being in control; timing meals to the benefit of your daily schedule; you choosing what foods you will eat; and you defusing the binge-trigger trick by defatting the food being "secretly" suggested.

- Always practice the compromise tactic *only when needed* and always simultaneously with other personal tactics. I define *only when needed* as the extreme point that you know is your threshold or breaking point. Your program is not designed to hurt you or to make you feel like you are entering a torture chamber. Your compromise tactic is one of the ways out of such thoughts. It is also one personal tactic your Fat Self may try to steal right out from under you if you do not support it by practicing other personal tactics at the same time.

- Your Fat Self will express its attitude toward food and its role in your life in myriad ways, and all of them carry the same message: there is no real connection between what you eat and how you look or feel about yourself. You may feel physically uncomfortable or emotionally distraught because you overate, but your Fat Self considers these feelings of discomfort only temporary and a small "price" to pay for the pleasure of eating with abandon. Even if you think you may gain weight as a consequence, you will not *believe* it, because you cannot see or even feel the added pounds in the foods you are eating. To reverse this unrealistic attitude, remember this: those added pounds are not temporary, nor can they be wished away.

- Practice your personal trick tactics in response to *your* desire to overeat, not mine. For example, if TV food commercials don't bother you, but the sound of your twelve-year-old chomping a peanut-butter sandwich sends you racing for the loaf of bread, try picturing peanut butter rotting the roof of your mouth instead of just sticking to it. Or, instead of responding to the sound of eating a fat food, reverse the sound to that of eating thin, and reach for a raw vegetable or fresh fruit snack instead.

Special Occasions

The real struggle in dieting is an inner one, but there are certain occasions—scenes of confrontation—that seem to increase that struggle. However, you can use these occasions as opportunities to practice your personal diet tactics.

The Cocktail Hour

Especially for the working person, "happy hour" can mean a special time for socializing and relaxing after a hard day. It can also mean a stomach congested with hundreds of calories from liquor and hors d'oeuvres. What do you do?

If you can drink moderately while dieting, do so. If not, you drink nonalcoholic drinks like a Virgin Mary, mineral water, coffee, or club soda with a lime twist. If your favorite after-work gathering place serves only high-calorie canapés, ask the manager to change the menu, or find another place that is more in step with your needs. Or, simply stay away until your Thin Self is stronger and healthier.

Holidays Made for Feasting

It has been said that holidays can be the loneliest times for some people. Holidays can also be very difficult for people who are dieting. Everyone else gets to eat, and you feel deprived; you might even be tempted to use this as a binge trigger.

Your Fat Self will have a heyday with your thoughts and feelings about yourself. It will chide you at one minute for being so fat, and cuddle up the next by telling you you have a right to feel sorry for yourself. Meanwhile, it will begin plotting the next binge.

You can handle these holidays by disarming the weapon. While others are feasting on fat foods, you observe the holiday by strengthening *yourself*. Plan the menu with normal thin-portion servings, do the shopping, even set the table. Invite only those friends and loved ones who support your undertaking, and in general surround yourself with those who will not sabotage you.

If someone else is doing the cooking, make sure he or she includes some foods that are on your diet. When you sit down to dinner, eat thin-size portions. And for heaven's sake, take one bite of every dish served, to reverse your Fat Self's power play of trying to make you feel deprived.

I know this is easier said than done. Some of you spend holidays with your families, and you know you can't count on support from people who may have been responsible for many of your Fat Self's habits in the first place. In fact, they may even attempt to undermine your resolve. If this is the case, try to prepare yourself with personal tactics that affirm your thinning perspective.

Home Alone on a Saturday Night

Believe it or not, there are lots of thin people who don't have dates every weekend. However, they do not use these occasions to feel lonely, unwanted, socially ostracized, or sexually rejected. Nor do they use nights alone as binge triggers.

Again, you can disarm your Fat Self's "secret" trigger finger by defatting the occasion itself. Make plans to spend time with supportive friends, and then carry out these plans. Also, take a look at the activities you enjoy (besides eating)—the things you're good at or that make you feel proud. What's stopping you from doing them? You can let your Fat Self trick you into sitting in isolation with nothing to do but eat. Or, you can (if you have to) pick yourself up and start actively participating in your own life and those of others around you. Your Fat Self will not like your moving out of isolation. But you will.

Taking It Off and Getting Comfortable

Often, the best floor show in town is your Fat Self's feeling of freedom when you take off your clothes and slip into your favorite loose-fitting house robe. "Now," your Fat Self says, "let's get comfortable. Sit down. Let's get down to some real relaxation after a horrible day. And let's do some serious eating." But think about it: If there are no clothes constraining your body, there are no reminders of how large you are. When you put on that muumuu, you are putting on far more than a comfortable feeling.

Does this mean you have to get rid of your favorite fleeces, soft terries, or fluffy flannels, or that you can't change into "something comfortable" ever again? Certainly not! There are form-fitting robes, lounging attire that clings to your newly developing curves, and jogging suits made of soft cotton jersey that fit your body and still permit a full range of movement.

One of your Fat Self's favorite tricks is to hide your body in loose-fitting garments. Trick it right back. Maintain your comfort, but do it with style. Have two or three fitted lounging outfits in colors that make you feel happy or remind you of spring or fall, nature's own seasons of transformation.

When you do come home from work, set a new ritual for getting comfortable by doing even more than changing your clothes. Take the time (steal it at first, if you have to) to get into a hot bath or a brisk shower to soak out some of the day's tension. Sing to yourself affirmations of how well you take care of your body and how you feel about it.

Making Your Personal Diet Tactics Work

All of your personal diet tactics work on the basis of *time, consistency, and practice*, which habituate your actions and your attitudes. Your Fat Self has used these three techniques well in establishing fat food habits that keep you overweight. Your Thin Self can learn to use these habituating techniques too.

Your personal diet tactics, like your new thin food habits, are conscious actions and attitudes; you practice them with full awareness. There is nothing automatic about them when you first begin practicing them. You have to think about them constantly, and that takes hard work. But when you practice thin food habits and your personal diet tactics consistently, they do, over time, become automatic and replace your other, fat food habits.

The decision is always up to you, the designer of your personal program, as to which food desire you will fulfill. Consistency is achieved through practice. And practice does take time. But remember, you have the rest of your life ahead of you.

CHAPTER SIX

Food Suggestions

I RAN INTO A SOLID wall of resistance the day I began planning my personal food menus. I had been feeling excited and confident, ready to end the preparation phase and begin the diet itself. Therefore, I was shocked when I realized that I did not want to plan my own menus. I did not know how, nor did I want to learn.

In my previous diets, the menus and calorie counts were provided for me; all I had to do was to follow the instructions religiously. Unquestionably, such diet programs had been very convenient. However, they had taught me nothing about nutrition.

What I needed now was to learn the calorie contents and other nutritional benefits of the foods I had been eating all my life (and would continue eating for the rest of it), not the foods somebody else told me to eat *while dieting*. I had to calculate the nutritional values of all the foods I ate, then to decide whether each item would help or hinder my efforts to lose weight permanently.

I already knew how to stay fat; my Fat Self had taught me well. What I lacked was the knowledge of how to stay thin. Without adequate understanding of nutrition, there would be no permanent weight loss.

The first thing I learned about nutrition was that the human body needs more than forty nutrients in order to maintain physical health. When you consume foods that contain adequate amounts of vitamins, minerals, water, proteins, carbohydrates, and fats, you are eating a balanced diet. I was delighted to realize that of these, only three groups contain calories.

Let's take a closer look at each of these six nutrient groups.

- *Vitamins* are organic chemicals found in fresh foods. They help form enzymes that are necessary to process other nutrients. Some are water-soluble: C, folic acid, B_1, B_2, niacin, B_6, B_{12}, biotin, and pantothenic acid. Others are fat-soluble: A, D, E, and K. The difference between water- and fat-soluble vitamins is that the former dissolve in water that is present in the digestive tract before being absorbed for use by the body, while the latter dissolve in fat nutrients that are present in the digestive tract.
- *Minerals* are inorganic substances found initially in the air and soil, then absorbed into plants. We in turn eat the plants, or the animals that have eaten the plants, or both. Minerals, like vitamins, help to form enzymes. They also perform other important functions within the body: enable electrical conduction to take place, help to distribute water, and participate in controlling heat build-up. There are twenty-five minerals essential to good health. Eating a variety of foods helps ensure that you will get them.
- *Water* has been called the most important nutrient of all, because life is not possible without it. Its metabolic function is to transport all the other nutrients inside the body where needed. Of the five pints needed daily, you usually get three pints from beverages and the other two from foods that contain water.
- *Proteins* are caloric nutrients. They contain 4 calories per gram and are made up of amino acids, which are the building blocks of body tissue. Of the twenty-one amino acids necessary for good health, nine must come

from the foods you eat, as your body cannot manufacture them.

Amino acids come from two different kinds of protein. The first is animal protein—meat, fish, poultry, eggs, and milk products—and it contains all nine essential amino acids. Vegetable proteins (found in leafy vegetables, potatoes, corn, nuts, cereals, and grains) lack one or more of the essential nine amino acids. However, by combining vegetable proteins with those found in other foods, you can get all nine essential amino acids.

- *Carbohydrates* are caloric nutrients. They contain 4 calories per gram and are made up of three kinds of sugars: monosaccharides (like glucose and fructose, found in fruits and honey); disaccharides (like lactose, found in milk, and sucrose, which is granulated table sugar); and polysaccharides, which are multiple sugars.

Polysaccharides come in two forms: starch and fiber. Starches are made up of millions of sugar molecules, which easily break down into simple sugars before they are absorbed by the body. Fiber is also made up of sugar molecules, but these polysaccharide sugars, called "complex carbohydrates," cannot easily be broken down and absorbed for energy use. Instead, most of them pass through the body, absorbing water and some fat along the way. Fresh fruits, vegetables, whole grains, and cereals contain a lot of fiber. Fiber is an excellent diet food, as it gives you a full feeling but does not have excessively high calories.

Carbohydrates are the body's most efficient fuel for energy. They provide energy for both muscles and the brain. Indeed, the brain is fueled almost exclusively by glucose, a monosaccharide.

- *Fats* are the highest-calorie nutrients. They contain 9 calories per gram and are made up of fatty acids. Like carbohydrates, they provide a great deal of energy. Like protein, they have tissue-building properties. Like vitamins and minerals, they help the body use other nutrients. For example, fat-soluble vitamins cannot be absorbed and utilized by the body without the presence of fat.

Unfortunately, most people prefer the taste of fatty foods to any other. Fats are essential for good health, though unquestionably in far smaller quantities than are currently consumed, especially by Americans.

Caloric Values of Nutrients

Calories, according to *Webster's New Collegiate Dictionary*, are an "energy-producing value in food when oxidized in the body." In other words, calories provide the energy on which the body runs. You cannot live without them.

Calories have fixed values (like 4 calories per gram of carbohydrate or 9 calories per gram of fat) and relative values in terms of how densely they are packed into individual foods.

For example, four ounces of red snapper contain 105 calories, 22 grams of protein, and 1 gram of fat. Four ounces of butter contain 812 calories, 1 gram of protein, and 92 grams of fat. Both of these foods weigh a quarter of a pound, but the butter, which contains 92 grams of fat, definitely has more calories than the fish, which contains only 1 gram of fat.

Eventually I learned to use butter in teaspoons instead of quarter-pounds. I also learned that instead of butter, with its 35 calories per teaspoon, I could have any of the following foods for about the same number of calories:

- ¾ cup steamed broccoli sprinkled with lemon juice
- 1 cucumber
- ½ small white potato, baked, boiled, or steamed
- 1½ cups zucchini
- 1 small peach

Needless to say, I was delighted with my discoveries. I learned that by selecting the right foods, I could not only eat more, but I could select from a greater variety of foods to make up the 800 calories I would be eating every day.

I also learned how nutritious bananas are. I had avoided them on previous diets because I thought they were high in calories compared to other fruits. However, one medium banana only has 20 calories more than a medium apple, but a lot more potassium. When I compared one medium banana with one tablespoon of mayonnaise, which I used to eat in large quantities, I found this:

One medium-sized banana (6.3 ounces) has 100 calories, .2 grams of fat, and 26 grams of carbohydrate. One tablespoon of mayonnaise has 103 calories, 11 grams of fat, .1 grams of carbohydrate.

Since carbohydrates are more nutritious than fats and are also primary sources for many vitamins and minerals, I included them often in my diet. However, carbohydrates, or any other single nutrients, are not sufficient by themselves. We need nutrients from all six groups. Dr. Wilson recommended that for dieting purposes, each day's menu should contain the following nutrient percentages: proteins: 40–45%; carbohydrates: 30–35%; fats: 15–20%.

Nutrition Goals

The above percentages reflect good nutrition while dieting. To help me translate these numbers into real foods, I used a summary of *Dietary Goals for the United States*, the report of the U.S. Senate's Select Committee on Nutrition and Human Needs. This report gave me guidelines for challenging my Fat Self's food preferences and for drawing up my own basic food list.

First, I listed what I had to do to meet my current nutrition needs, as follows:

1. Select basic foods and beverages for maximum nutritional value with minimum calories.

2. Select a variety of foods rich in vitamins and minerals.
3. Eat calories rather than drink them, like oranges rather than orange juice. Milk, an important source of animal protein, would be an exception.
4. Select fresh fruits, vegetables, whole grains, and cereals high in fiber.

List of Personal Nutrition Goals

- Eat recommended 4-ounce servings of fresh meat, fish, and poultry, eliminating high-fat cuts like porterhouse, rib steaks, and hamburger.
- Increase daily portions of fresh fruits and low-starch vegetables.
- Eat whole grains and whole-grain cereals, which have not had all their nutrients milled out of them.
- Replace whole milk and whole-milk products with low- and nonfat selections.
- Decrease sodium intake by using spices, herbs, and salt substitutes.
- Replace bottled oils with spray oils like Pam, which has only 3 calories per 1.25 seconds of spraying time.
- Cook with Teflon-coated pans.

Basic Food Groups and Portion Sizes

In 1954, the U.S. Department of Agriculture devised the Four Food Groups categorization system. Its purpose was to simplify daily meal selection while ensuring adequate amounts of nutrients from selections within each group.

USDA Four Food Groups

Group	Nutrients
1. Meats and Meat Alternatives (like poultry, fish, eggs, peanut butter)	Protein Fat Vitamins: B_1, B_{12}, niacin, pantothenic acid Mineral: iron
2. Milk and Milk Products (like yoghurt and cottage cheese)	Protein Fat Vitamin: B_2 Mineral: calcium
3. Fruits and Vegetables	Carbohydrates Vitamins: A, C, biotin, folic acid
4. Breads and Cereals	Carbohydrates Proteins Vitamins: B_1, B_6, E, niacin Mineral: iron

The USDA, one of the best sources for nutrition information, also identified the following serving sizes (for average-size Americans) to meet nutritional needs:

Food	Portion Size	Portions (per day for adults)
	Meat Group	2
meat, fish and poultry	3 ounces cooked (4 ounces raw)	
eggs	2	
	Milk Group	2
milk	8 ounces	
cheese	1¼ ounces	
yoghurt, plain	8 ounces	
	Fruit and Vegetable Group	4
fruit, cut up	½ cup	
vegetable, cut up	½ cup	

Bread and Cereal Group		4
bread	1 slice	
rice	½ cup, cooked	
cooked cereal	½ cup	

After reviewing my prediet food preferences and habits listed in the Record Keeping section of my large spiral notebook, I realized it was time to add a new section: "Food Suggestions."

I decided to expand the government's food groups by three, and to make other changes as well. My system of food categorization formed my Basic Food List.

Basic Food List

Group 1: Meats and Meat Alternatives
Group 2: Milk and Milk Products
Group 3: Vegetables
Group 4: Fruits
Group 5: Whole Grains and Cereals
Group 6: Visible Fats
Group 7: Snacks

I now had seven major food groups. In order to turn this list into 800-calorie daily menus, I had first to select for each heading a variety of specific foods that would meet my nutritional needs. Then I had to calculate the calorie content of each selection, the portion size, and the cooking technique to be used. Finally, I had to determine how many calories I would need from each group to meet Dr. Wilson's recommended nutrient percentages.

Basing Food Selection on Personal Preference

My decision to depart from the USDA's format and base my food selections on personal preference proved vital in helping me overcome my Fat Self's resistance to "diet foods." Since my Fat Self loved chicken, milk, eggs, bread, and potatoes, it raised no objections to my continuing to eat them.

In making the selections for each food group, I made under each heading a separate list of foods I was accustomed to eating.

Under meat, for example, I listed these prediet favorites: hamburger, bacon, fatty steak, bologna, chicken with skin, hot dogs, fried eggs, liver, and fatty pork chops. Then I looked up the calories for these and blanched. I knew, from monitoring my prediet food habits, that I had "secretly" selected the highest-calorie meats I could find. Hot dogs and the cheaper cuts of hamburger, for example, contain more than 75 percent fat. I was in trouble with my prediet cooking techniques as well as portion sizes: I always fried my usual two half-pound hamburger patties, and always ate my three to four hot dogs in one sitting.

I had variety in selection, but it was variety in fat first, animal protein second. Clearly, I was out of control when it came to meat selections. I rewrote the list, eliminating the high-fat meats as follows:

Group 1: Meat, and Meat Alternatives

Item Portion	Calories
round steak, lean, 4 ounces raw, broiled	214
tuna fish, 1 6½-ounce can, packed in water	220
chicken breast, ½, skinned, broiled or steamed	155
beef liver, 4 ounces raw, cooked in Teflon pan with no oil	156

Group 2: Milk and Milk Products

My list of prediet milk preferences included whole milk, soft, creamy cheeses, and ice cream. Not much of a selection, and all laden with fat.

My new list reflected my new perspective toward this second food group.

Item	Portion	Calories
nonfat milk		
	8 ounces for drinking	90
	1/4 cup for cereal	23
nonfat plain yoghurt		
	1/4 cup for eating	31
	1 tablespoon for sauces	8
low-fat cottage cheese		
	1/2 cup for eating	100
	1 tablespoon for sauces	13
hard cheddar cheese		
	1 ounce for eating	105
	1 tablespoon, grated	20

I had always considered cottage cheese a diet food and had not liked it, but I put it on my list because it is a good animal-protein source (with all nine essential amino acids), and it has the added benefit of requiring no preparation. I knew there would be times when I would still want or need fast foods, and I was beginning to learn that fast foods did not have to be fat foods.

I did not initially like nonfat plain yoghurt, but I chose to acquire a taste for that, too. I planned to make it my number-one thin-food replacement for butter, oil, and mayonnaise.

Group 3: Vegetables

Making vegetable selections proved difficult for me. I had always eaten the canned or frozen varieties, and generally the high-starch kinds like lima beans, peas, and corn. But the more familiar I became with fresh vegetables and new preparation techniques, like steaming instead of boiling, and having cut-up raw vegetables for snacks instead of pretzels or potato chips, the more I came to enjoy them.

I did not eliminate high-starch vegetables, because they are high-fiber foods; I did reduce my portions, though.

To further expand my knowledge about vegetables, I made up three vegetable lists: "High-Starch Vegetables," "Low-

Starch Vegetables," and "Raw Vegetables for Salads and Snacks." I distinguished high- from low-starch vegetables based on carbohydrate content. If half a cup of vegetables contained fewer than 10 grams of carbohydrate, it made the "low" list. Here are samples from these lists:

High Starch Vegetables

Item	Portion	Calories	Carbohydrates (grams)
kidney beans, cooked	¼ cup	55	9.9
lima beans, fordhooks	¼ cup	51.5	9.35
corn	¼ cup	35	8
lentils, cooked	¼ cup	54	10
peas	¼ cup	29	5
white potato	1 small	90	23

Low-Starch Vegetables (fresh, steamed)

Item	Portion	Calories	Carbohydrates (grams)
asparagus	4 spears	12	2
green beans	½ cup	16	3.3
beets	¼ cup	17	3.7
broccoli	½ cup	20	3.5
cabbage	½ cup	15	3.1
carrots	½ cup	25	5.8
cauliflower	½ cup	14	2.5
eggplant	½ cup	19	4.1

Raw Vegetables for Salads and Snacks

Item	Portion	Calories	Carbohydrates (grams)
green beans	1 ounce	8	1.8
broccoli	1 ounce	7	1.3
carrots	½ medium	10	2.4

cauliflower	1 ounce	8	1.5
celery	1/2 stalk	4	.8
cucumber	6 slices	8	1
lettuce	1/4 head	15	3.3
mushrooms	1/2 cup	10	1.5
onions	1/2 cup	21	5
green pepper	1/2 average	7	1.5
radishes	1/2 cup	10	2.1
tomato	1/2 small	15	4
zucchini	1/2 cup	9	2

Group 4: Fruits

I selected my fruits the same way I selected my vegetables. My prediet preferences had been for the canned-in-heavy-syrup variety.

Now I learned that by switching to fresh fruits, I added both fiber and natural vitamins to my diet. In addition, I discovered an unexpected bonus: When I cut or sliced whole fruits into bite-sized pieces, I increased the number of sides or surface areas, which greatly increased the taste of the fruit. For example, I would peel a navel orange and separate the sections, then cut each section into three small pieces. Instead of ending up with one whole orange to be eaten in perhaps ten bites, I experienced the taste of that orange thirty-three times.

By increasing my sense of taste along with the number of times I experienced each taste, I learned to appreciate the taste of food rather than its quantity.

Here are samples from the fourth food group on my Basic Food List:

Item	Portion	Calories
apple, spears or slices	1/2 medium	40
banana, spears or slices	1/3 medium	33
cantaloupe, wedge	1/4 melon	29
pink grapefruit, sections	1/2 grapefruit	46
grapes	1/4 cup	28
orange	1/2	30

peach, spears or slices	1/2	17
pear, spears or slices	1/4	25
pineapple, sliced or chopped	1/2 cup	36
raisins	1 tablespoon	36

Group 5: Whole Grains and Cereals

My prediet preferences included cake, cookies, dough-nuts, and extra-large slices of soft white bread. The first three preferences were easy to let go of because of their high refined-sugar content without benefit of high fiber.

However, bread was my nemesis, and I was reluctant to put it on my new list, fearing that my Fat Self would use it as a binge trigger. As I read more about it, though, I decided that one slice of stone-ground whole wheat bread each day would be beneficial, as it is high in protein, rich in fiber, and very nutritious.

Here are some examples from the fifth food group on my list:

Item	Portion	Calories
Bread		
whole wheat	1 slice	60
plain bagel	1/2	81
small pita	1/2	63
9" flour tortilla	1	169
Cooked Cereal		
oatmeal (rolled oats), dry	1/4 cup	110
Whole Grains		
barley, dry	1 tablespoon	43
bulgur, dry	1 ounce	100
pasta, cooked	1/2 cup	78
white rice, cooked	1/2 cup	90

Group 6: Visible Fats

I called this group "Visible Fats" because I could see them as I added them to other foods—like butter and mayonnaise added to bread, or oil added to salads or cooking pans. These fats were not already present in foods but were added to enhance taste and texture.

Visible fats are condiments, not basic foods. Therefore, their portions are usually small. Unfortunately, I had the pre-diet habits of buying foods with hidden high-fat nutrients and eating visible fats in food-size portions.

I decided now to use no visible fats during my diet. This did not mean I excluded essential fat nutrients: I got more than enough of them in meat, chicken, and milk products. As a matter of fact, all animal proteins contain fat nutrients; even nonfat milk has traces of fat in it, as do low-starch vegetables.

Having made this decision, I now drew up a list of no-calorie and low-calorie sauces, spreads, and seasonings, which appears in the appendix.

I did a lot of experimenting with these taste enhancers, and eventually I overcame my Fat Self's desire for butter, oil, and mayonnaise.

Group 7: Snacks

I made snacks an integral part of my food list because they had always been an integral part of my life. I did, however, change the calorie contents by replacing fat snacks with thin ones.

Part of my Fat Self's attitude toward snacking while dieting was an anticipated absence of taste. I replaced this attitude with my thinning perspective by selecting my snacks from a wide array of low-calorie foods. I surrounded my carrot sticks with other raw vegetables, and I added bits of fruit to further enhance taste.

Both fresh fruits and raw vegetables are carbohydrates. In small amounts eaten between meals, they served as energy picker-uppers due to their natural sugars, as stomach stuffers due to their dietary fiber, and, equally important, as sources for natural vitamins and minerals.

Turning Nutrient Percentages Into Calories

Finally, I turned my Basic Food List into the following 800-calorie plan with the help of Nancy Wilson, a registered dietician.

Group 1:   Meat and Meat Alternatives—200 calories
Group 2:   Milk and Milk Products—100 calories
Group 3:   Vegetables—150 calories
Group 4:   Fruits—150 calories
Group 5:   Whole Grains and Cereals—150 calories
Group 6:   Visible Fats—0 (during Phase One and Two only)
Group 7:   Snacks—50 calories

Drawing Up Personal Menus

To draw up personal menus, I had first to decide on the number of meals I would eat per day, and then select the specific foods to be included, making sure that I did not exceed the recommended number of calories for each group.

I decided to eat three meals daily, plus one or two snacks, and to eat them at "regular" mealtimes and intervals throughout the day, to meet my body's energy requirements.

In making my selections from each food group, I had only to choose the items I wanted and make sure that they totaled the recommended number of calories for that group.

I also used personal diet tactics in planning my menus. For example, I included high-fiber foods in all three meals and snacks to give me a well-fed feeling, which helped counter my Fat Self's feelings of deprivation and constant hunger. I also included specific items in each meal that took time to prepare as well as time to eat, thus countering my old hurry-up attitude at meals. Finally, by taking the time and care to draw up my personal menus, I was strengthening my Thin Self and learning more about how to live thin.

In the appendix you will find my menus for all three phases, plus observation notes and calorie calculations. While it is all right for you to follow my menus, I believe that you will be more successful if you draw up your own, taking into account your personal food preferences and habits.

The time and energy you spend in acquiring essential food knowledge as you plan your menus will help ensure your living thin permanently.

How to Prepare Your Basic Food List

Drawing up your Basic Food List can be hard work, because you must learn not only the nutritional values (including calories) of the foods you will be eating on your diet, but those of the foods you ate prediet. And that means exposing your Fat Self's control over your food. When you draw up your Basic Food List, you are taking a step toward regaining that control.

Identifying Your Nutrition Goals

Simply writing the calorie and nutrient values alongside each food item on your list is not sufficient. To identify your personal nutrition goals, you must learn what nutritional balance is. I suggest you read the first chapter in *Jane Brody's Nutrition Book*, "The New Nutrition: You Are What You Eat." For quick reference to essential nutrients, I recommend *What's In What You Eat*, by Will Eisner, published by Bantam Books.

Once you have identified your personal nutrition goals, make a new section in your large notebook for "Food Suggestions" and write down these goals.

Categorizing Your Prediet Food Preferences

You have already identified your prediet food preferences in your habit-observation exercises. Now you will list those preferences under the same seven food-group headings that I used:

Group 1:   Meats and Meat Alternatives
Group 2:   Milk and Milk Products
Group 3:   Vegetables
Group 4:   Fruits
Group 5:   Whole Grains and Cereals
Group 6:   Visible Fats
Group 7:   Snacks

Alongside each prediet item you list under these groups, identify the portion size you now eat and how you cook it. Next, use your calorie counter to calculate how many calories are contained in the item and its nutrient value in terms of carbohydrates and/or fats, and record these numbers. (Do not forget to double the calorie and nutrient numbers if your portion size is double that listed in your calorie counter.)

Following are some recommendations to help you complete your prediet lists:

- List only those foods you eat daily, weekly, or at least once a month.
- List all the parts of each food you eat. For example, if you usually eat both the meat and the fat or skin around it, list both.
- When listing visible fats (butter, margarine, cooking oils, and mayonnaise), first list the food you add the fat to, then identify how much fat you add. For example, if you eat pancakes, how much oil do you cook them in, and how much butter do you put on top of them? If you make tuna-fish salad, how much mayonnaise do you use?
- Fruit juices belong under Group 4: Fruits.
- Milk shakes, chocolate milk, and frozen yoghurt belong under the milk group.
- Nuts like cashews, peanuts, and peanut butter should be listed under Group 1, for they are considered meat

alternatives, as are eggs, because of their high protein content.

- Dried peas and beans are legumes; list them under Group 3: Vegetables.
- Grains and cereals include breads, biscuits, cookies, cakes, muffins, pasta, pancakes, rice, bulgur wheat, breakfast cereals (hot and cold), hominy grits, crackers, and barley.
- Soda pop, candy bars, chocolate, popcorn, and alcoholic beverages belong under Group 7: Snacks. Even though you may also eat cookies, apples, potato chips, and sausage sticks as snacks, each of these items has its own food group.
- If you eat mostly processed foods, you are eating a lot of hidden sugar and salt (usually listed as sodium in processed food). Use Will Eisner's *What's In What You Eat* to identify the salt content of processed foods.

Making Your Food Selections from Your Prediet Preferences

In order for a prediet item to make your Basic Food List, you must reduce its calories while retaining its nutritional benefit. Of course, calories can always be reduced by merely cutting the portion size. But you want to do more than simply cut calories: you want to learn to live thin for the rest of your life. The following step-by-step instructions show you how.

Group 1: Meat and Meat Alternatives

Turn to the Group 1 prediet list in your large notebook. Look at the first item, noting the quantity you usually eat, how you prepare it, and how many calories and grams of fat it has. Now use your calorie counter to determine the calories and grams of fat for half of your "normal" portion, *for meat only, no fat or skin.* For example, if your prediet list has an entry for two 3½-ounce loin lamb chops "pan broiled" in a tablespoon of

98

oil, and you ate both the meat and the fat rimming it, you were consuming 720 calories (124 from the oil) and 72 grams of fat (14 from the oil). If you want to include lamb chops on your Basic Food List, you must cut your portion to one chop, eat the meat only, and broil it, without oil. Your lean selection has 120 calories and fewer than 6 grams of fat.

Your prediet preferences may have included hot dogs, cheap cuts of hamburger, bacon, salami, bologna, and spare-ribs. These meats contain at least 75 percent fat. Since this fat content cannot be changed, you can reduce the number of calories in these foods only by reducing your portion size. However, remember that these meats are not very nutritious. I recommend that you *not* include them in your Basic Food List.

Group 2: Milk and Milk Products

You can reduce calories in this group by switching from whole milk and related products to low- or nonfat varieties. If you already prefer the low- or nonfat items, simply copy them over from your prediet list to your Basic Food List.

If you use heavy cream, half and half, or sour cream in cooking, switch over to low-fat milk, low- or nonfat plain yoghurt, or low-fat buttermilk.

If soft, creamy cheeses are listed as prediet preferences, calculate their nutritional contents, then compare them with the corresponding values for hard cheeses made with low- or nonfat milk. Only hard cheeses should be included in your Basic Food List.

Milk shakes, ice cream, pudding, chocolate milk, and frozen yoghurt must not be included in your Basic Food List, regardless of portion sizes. Both the fat and sugar contents of these foods are simply too high.

Group 3: Vegetables

Vegetables have their maximum nutritional value when fresh and raw. Their calorie contents don't change much when you boil or steam them, but their nutritional benefits do change: lightly steamed vegetables retain more nutrients than boiled ones.

Calorie contents do change with other cooking techniques. Both pan-frying and stir-frying, for example, require cooking oil, which of course increases the number of calories. Deep-fried batter-dipped vegetables have even more calories.

As you inspect your prediet vegetable preferences, think about how you can cut calories without cutting nutritional benefits. Like me, you may want to make up three separate lists of vegetables according to calorie range (see p. 91–92), which is determined by starch, or carbohydrate, content.

Do not be afraid to eat high-starch vegetables. Remember, carbohydrates are your body's most efficient fuel for energy. However, since they contain more calories than do the low-starch vegetables, put them on your Basic Food List in lean quarter-cup portions.

Your salads-and-snacks list will contain many of the same items as your low-calorie–low-starch list, but in smaller portions. I recommend making a duplicate of this list to tape up in your kitchen for quick reference when you're making a salad or vegetable snack.

Remember that in making lean vegetable selections, you need not cut taste along with calories. Herbs, spices, lemon juice, pieces of fruit, other vegetables, wine with the alcohol cooked out, and low- or nonfat plain yoghurt all enhance taste without adding calories.

Group 4: Fruits

Fruits, like meats, come in a variety of forms. There's dried fruit, canned-in-heavy-syrup fruit, and fruit that comes in pies, tarts, mousses, and inside doughnuts. If these items appear on your prediet preference list, leave them there. When you compare their calorie, fat, and sugar contents to the corresponding values for fresh fruits, you will understand immediately why they must not make your Basic Food List.

Although fruit that is canned in water or its own juice has fewer calories than the canned-in-heavy-syrup variety, it is far less nutritious than fresh fruit.

Fruit juices have the advantage over canned fruit in that, usually, no extra sugar is added to them. However, juices do not have the fiber that fresh fruits have.

Consider these factors as you decide where to cut calories while retaining maximum nutrition in the fruit group.

Group 5: Whole Grains and Cereals

I found it not only difficult but painful at first to switch from sugar-coated cornflakes to hot oatmeal made from cooked rolled oats. The taste, texture, and temperature weren't the only differences, though. Although these two cereals contain basically the same number of calories, my cornflakes had far less protein, calcium, phosphorus, and potassium—and far more carbohydrates—than does my hot oatmeal.

As with cereals, soft white breads contain basically the same number of calories as do their whole-grain counterparts. However, the whole-grain varieties, made from stone-ground flour, have retained most of their nutrient values, including a large amount of vegetable protein and dietary fiber.

Pasta, rice, and grains like bulgur and wheat berry also have large amounts of vegetable protein and dietary fiber. If these items are already on your preference list, simply reduce their portions before adding them to your Basic Food List.

Regardless of portion size, muffins, croissants, cakes, and cookies should not be transferred from your prediet preference list to your Basic Food List. They contain too much fat and sugar and not enough of the essential nutrients.

Do not make the mistake of thinking that whole grains and cereals are "too high" in calories. Many of these grains and cereals in combination with other grains and certain vegetables make complete meals that provide all nine essential amino acids; therefore, they are alternatives to meat dishes.

In other words, while many whole grains and cereals contain more calories than do "diet foods," they are lean selections because of their nutritional value.

Group 6: Visible Fats

If you can use butter, margarine, oils, and mayonnaise in moderate amounts (teaspoonfuls), you may put them on your Basic Food List. If you tend to go overboard with these items, however, I suggest that you *not* include them, at least during the weight-loss phases of your diet.

Group 7: Snacks

Many of us are accustomed to snacking on refined-sugar and/or fat-rich foods, or to turning a simple snack into a full meal or several in one sitting. But you needn't say "no" to snacking to correct these bad habits.

When you make selections for this final food group, you will think "thin foods," and you now have two excellent sources from which to draw: your vegetable list for salads and snacks, and fresh-fruit list. For even more variety, add items from Group 2: Milk and Milk Products—but remember to use snack-size portions.

From Basic Food List to Your Personal Menus

Once you have completed your Basic Food List, select the total-calorie plan you intend to follow while losing weight. Write the recommended calories for each food group on your list. The recommended nutrient percentages have been translated into actual calories per food group by Nancy Wilson, R.D., as follows.

Three Basic Personal Food-Plan Diets

		800 Plan	800 Plan*	1000 Plan	1200 Plan
Group 1:	Meats and Meat Alternatives	200	200	200	200
Group 2:	Milk and Milk Products	100	100	100	100
Group 3:	Vegetables	150	150	200	300
Group 4:	Fruits	150	100	200	200
Group 5:	Whole Grains and Cereals	150	150	200	300
Group 6:	Visible Fats	0	50	50	50
Group 7:	Snacks	50	50	50	50

*This 800 plan has 50 visible-fat calories and 100 fruit calories.

In drawing up personal menus for Phase One, you must decide the number of meals per day you will eat and the specific items you will include in each meal, making certain that you do not exceed recommended portions or the total daily calorie limit.

I recommend that you also plan three daily meals—breakfast, lunch, and dinner—plus one or two snacks. Regularly scheduled meals help you restore calorie control and practice good habits, provide food for your energy needs throughout your waking hours, when your body is most active, and aid the comfort and efficiency of your digestive system.

You now know the recommended number of calories for each of your food groups. Select items and portions that *approximate* these numbers. For example, suppose you select the alternate 800-calorie plan, which recommends 50 visible-fat calories. If you use one pat of butter, which contains 30 calories, you have 20 visible-fat calories left over. Simply add those 20 calories to your meat selection for that day, or to another group's selection. However, do not take "leftover" calories from any food groups to increase visible-fat and/or refined-sugar consumption.

I recommend drawing up personal menus for at least the

first seven days of your diet. Be sure to vary selections from one day to another and from one meal to another. Eating a variety of foods will help you stave off feelings of boredom, which is part of your Fat Self's diet mentality to sabotage your diet.

PART TWO

The Three-Phase Personal Food-Plan Diet

CHAPTER SEVEN

Phase One: Beginning Weight Loss

THE GOAL OF PHASE ONE is to replace fat foods and habits with thin ones.

You will now begin practicing the thin-food habits you observed while watching others and yourself during preparation. *Do not expect perfection during the first few weeks of Phase One.* You develop habits by practicing them over time.

Do not expect immediate resistance to following your food plan, either. You have been preparing to replace fat foods with thin ones ever since you made your decision to live thin. Your anticipation and excitement over actually beginning to lose weight now will probably exceed the feelings of doubt and fear promoted by your Fat Self.

During the first week or two of Phase One, as you strictly adhere to your food plan, you can expect to find new pleasures in taste and in eating itself. The prediet feelings of guilt, shame, and anxiety over eating will be absent.

However, do not think that this means your Fat Self is absent. I made that mistake, until I realized that my Fat Self was merely lying low. It remained quiet as I discovered the joys of eating fiber-rich, low-calorie carbohydrates in unaccustomed quantities, salads that tasted crisp and fresh—not wilted from the weight of too much oil—fresh fruits, and lightly steamed potatoes and carrots, which were actually sweet. I did not feel overly hungry, nor did I miss the butter I was accustomed to smearing over almost everything; but what surprised me the most was how good everything tasted.

My exhilaration at weigh-in times further lulled me into the belief that I had finally conquered my Fat Self. I lost 11½ pounds during the first week. Of course, I knew that part of that loss was water: I had not lost 11½ pounds of pure body fat. I was undaunted, however. Nothing was going to rob me of my sense of accomplishment.

When I completed the first week of Phase One, I was so delighted with my progress that I decided to repeat the same seven-day menu. This time, however, everything was different when I weighed in. The differences were in both weight loss and my attitude. During the first week, I had weighed myself four times. The numbers were my rewards. During the second week, I hit the scale bright and early every day. I lost only 3½ pounds. However, that was 3½ pounds of body fat, not water. I was less than happy, because the numbers were not as dramatic as the first week's. But I was not devastated.

I cannot say the same for my Fat Self. Some kind of plot was hatching inside me; there was a feeling of unease, like the quiet before a storm.

The storm struck on the first day of my third week of dieting. The scale read 226 pounds—up ½ pound since the day before.

I felt goosebumps on my naked skin. I glanced in the medicine-cabinet mirror and caught a flicker of fear in my eyes. I left the bathroom and stood before my full-length mirror. I did not look like I had gained ½ pound. Then again, I didn't look like I had lost 15 of my 240 pounds, either. I still looked morbidly obese. I could feel my Fat Self shiver with pleasure at the realization.

I went through the day with determination in my step and

"100 pounds in six months" on my lips. I ate my three meals and my snacks. That ½-pound gain was nothing to get upset about. I knew that it was only because of the quantities of complex carbohydrates I'd been eating: the fiber was a big water absorber, and everything was simply working its way through my bowels. Fear, however, had gotten a hold on me.

It strengthened its grasp the following morning when I stepped on the scale. It now read 227 pounds. I'd gained another ½ pound.

That night, my Fat Self popped up in all her former glory. I had just finished cooking dinner for myself and a friend— broiled chicken with the skin removed, steamed broccoli, steamed cauliflower, and steamed white potatoes. I got out lemon juice, dill, and cracked pepper to sprinkle on my food. At the same time, I got out the butter I'd bought that afternoon for my friend's vegetables. Suddenly I knew I was in trouble. Our plates were side by side.

For me, butter was a deadly enemy, a binge trigger comparable to bread. It was now in my hands, poised above the two plates. The tension mounted. My legs seemed to turn to stone.

I was just about to give in to the urgings of my Fat Self when my friend walked into the kitchen, picked up both our plates, and took them to the table. I didn't eat the butter that night—and I learned a valuable lesson: my Fat Self was going to use diet-mentality fear and other intimidation tactics to attack my still relatively new thinning perspective. Therefore, I needed to strengthen my Thin Self.

Your Fat Self's resistance will probably be low at the beginning of Phase One. To prepare for the attacks sure to come, you must begin consistently practicing your personal diet tactics.

Self-Affirmation

In addition to feeling good about strictly adhering to your food plan and practicing thin food habits, openly acknowledge your positive feelings with the most positive word in the English language: "yes."

- "Yes, snacking on these raw vegetables really does take the edge off my hunger."
- "Yes, this low-calorie sauce does taste good."
- "Yes, my portion of fish does look small, and I will be too after eating it."
- "Yes, I do want to learn to live thin."

Other self-affirming tactics can be used when shopping and preparing foods. For example, while shopping, pick up a bouquet of fresh flowers or a magazine you've been wanting to read but haven't because you spent the money on desserts or other high-calorie foods. When you finish shopping, take extra time to arrange your fresh flowers or to read your new magazine. When you prepare foods, don't just stand at the chopping block with your kids scampering around you or the television keeping you company. Instead, create a more positive atmosphere. Put on music that lifts your spirits, and set the table with your best dinnerware.

Self-Discipline

While practicing your self-affirming strategy, you will probably hear a "no" response piping up from your Fat Self. You must then assume a parental role with your Fat Self and discipline it as you would an unruly child.

For example, suppose you are dining out with friends. When the waiter tells your group what's on the dessert menu, your Fat Self says "yes" to everything, while your Thin Self hasn't heard any dessert mentioned that fits in with your diet. You apply discipline not by saying "no" to dessert, but by reversing the high calories to low ones. You order fresh strawberries or other fruit, without cream, herbal tea with lemon or cinnamon, or espresso.

If your Fat Self begins to rebel and you can feel the internal tension mounting, do what most parents do in similar situations with a child preparing to throw a tantrum: Firmly say "no," or take your Fat Self bodily out of the restaurant.

Time

Prediet, your Fat Self controlled your food time, dictating not only what you ate but *when you ate it*. During Phase One, you begin to take back control of time by strictly adhering to your food plan. Your menus designate mealtimes as well as meal selections. When you stick to your menus day after day and week after week, you are not just forming new habits—you are learning a control technique. You can expect your Fat Self to resist giving up its control in this area.

Time is one of the most focused-on aspects of weight loss. Most dieters, myself included, think about adhering to calorie-controlled eating regimens in terms of Day 1, Day 2, or Week 3, and so on, and literally count the passing time like a prison sentence. The idea of marking time by numbers is to make it seem to go faster. But I did not want the time of eating thin ever to come to an end. For this reason, I decided to continue eating basically the same meals (with adjustments for market and season availability) week after week after week during my Phase One. It was one more way of taking control of my Fat Self.

I recommend that you make your initial seven-day supply of menus into your Phase One Any-Week Food Plan. In this manner you directly challenge your Fat Self's resistance to being controlled. By eating the same foods at the same times throughout Phase One, you are telling your Fat Self that you are now in control of your eating habits.

Weighing In

The strength of your thinning perspective will be tested when you weigh your food portions and yourself week after week. You can expect your Fat Self to try to help you "read" the numbers on both of your scales.

Weighing Foods

You must measure and weigh your food portions. Remember: recommended portions of meat, chicken, and fish are 4 ounces raw or 3 ounces cooked. Do not let your Fat Self sneak in an extra ounce of cooked portions by making you "forget" this.

Fresh vegetables and some legumes, whole grains, and cereals can be weighed before cooking. Certain foods can be prepared in more than one-portion servings and refrigerated for future meals. If you do cook ahead, be sure to determine the calories per portion of these foods *cooked*.

Weighing Yourself

The numbers on your food scale will not be as difficult to interpret as those on your bathroom scale. The factors that influence food weights are always consistent: half a cup of raw, sliced cauliflower weighs 41½ grams every time; half a cup cooked weighs 62½ grams. The difference in weight is due to water absorption during cooking.

The factors that influence your changing body weight, on the other hand, are not so consistent. These factors include:

- how much you weigh before you start losing weight
- how sluggish your metabolism is prediet and how quickly it adjusts to reduced calories and nutritionally balanced meals
- your body's own patterns of weight loss (these patterns differ from person to person and between males and females)
- the chemical processes, many of which are not yet fully understood, that make up the metabolism

Your body requires a certain number of calories for energy. Most women require between 1700 and 2400 calories daily; most men require between 2500 and 3100. (These numbers vary according to height, age, body-frame size, and amount of physical activity.)

When you begin eating fewer calories, your body makes up for it by burning calories that are stored inside you in the form of fat deposits. A pound of body fat equals approximately 3500 stored calories. You lose weight by literally burning up these stored calories. But not every dieter burns body-fat calories at the same rate or even with predictable consistency.

Therefore, the numbers on your bathroom scale will change, but not always the way you think they should. They will go down, sometimes quickly, other times slowly, occasionally not at all for brief periods of time. And if you are not accustomed to eating fresh fruits, vegetables, and whole grains and cereals, all high in dietary fiber, the numbers on your scale may even go up a little.

If this happens, do not panic. Above all, do not let your Fat Self "interpret" the numbers on your scale. These numbers do not reflect your metabolic process—they reflect the *results of that process*, and these results *take time to register*. Be assured: when you eat fewer calories than your body requires over a sustained period of time, your body *will* metabolize calories from your body fat to make up that deficiency.

Use this knowledge to strengthen your thinning perspective.

Concluding Phase One

After three months of spending time at the chopping block, weighing all my food, and recording in my Food Log every morsel I ate, I was getting tired and bored. I had lost 40 pounds—one-third of my weight-loss goal. But by now I was beginning to take for granted the decreasing numbers recorded on my Weigh-In Chart.

When I designed the personal food-plan diet to include two phases of weight loss, I did so because I knew I would experience boredom and tiredness; such feelings were part of the diet mentality of my Fat Self.

Chances are that you, too, will experience these feelings. Perhaps your Fat Self will begin urging you to quit the diet, or to begin sneaking in a few of your old, favorite fat foods.

If you experience these feelings before you have reached at least one-third of your weight-loss goal, *beware*. Your Fat Self knows you are losing weight and does not like it. Now is the time for you once again to make a conscious choice between living thin and staying fat. Instead of giving back control to your Fat Self, let your Thin Self be your guide in continuing to apply the personal diet tactics you've learned.

Only when you have reached one-third of your weight-loss goal is it time to conclude Phase One.

CHAPTER EIGHT

Phase Two: Continuing Weight Loss

THE GOAL OF PHASE TWO is to replace your diet mentality with your thinning perspective—that is, to change your attitude, as in Phase One you changed your food habits. In continuing to lose weight, you will encounter heavy resistance in the form of boredom, weight-loss plateaus, and seemingly insatiable hunger. Each of these, if manipulated by your Fat Self, is a potential diet wrecker.

Your diet mentality, controlled by your Fat Self, wants to attack or discredit your weight loss. It can foster the belief that diets don't work and calories don't count. It can also make you question your commitment to permanent weight loss, or distort the results you get when you compare your diet program with that of others. For example, your Fat Self might make you think that because it took me nine months to get through Phase Two, it will take you the same amount of time. Neatly obscured in this time comparison is the fact that I lost 78 pounds, while you may need to lose far less than that and therefore will take less time.

Your thinning perspective, on the other hand, is the attitude of your Thin Self. It results from and reflects your decision to learn how to live thin. With each accomplishment, your thinning attitude grows in strength and confidence, thus furthering your efforts to reach and maintain your ideal weight.

You cannot learn to maintain your weight loss unless your Thin Self is strong enough to dominate your perspective. This domination must be achieved during Phase Two; if it is not, your Fat Self may wear you down to the point of quitting the diet.

Overcoming Boredom and Its Disguises

Boredom can rob you of your enthusiasm to continue losing weight, or it can kill the diet by prompting you to return to eating fat foods.

Overweighters often think of diet boredom as pertaining strictly to food (apple pie, for example, is more "interesting" than a fresh apple). The dieter feels that if he could just eat something besides "diet food," dieting would not be so boring.

In fact, boredom is more than a feeling about food. It is an over-all negative attitude, and it can be disguised as other feelings that make you want to quit your diet.

Boredom disguised as anger and frustration
- Food-sameness overload: If you eat broiled chicken one more time, you'll scream.
- Underweighter envy: You're ready to strangle thin people who have to "overeat" to maintain normal weight.

Boredom disguised as low self-esteem and inadequacy
- The-grass-is-greener attitude: You lessen your self-worth by thinking that thin people have more because they don't have a weight problem.
- Detail glut: Paying attention to details—counting calories, remembering how many meals you've eaten, keeping up the entries in your Food Log—is difficult for you.

Boredom disguised as impatience
- Instant gratifier: If your desires are not instantly gratified, you're ready to switch to ones you believe will be.
- Fortitude failure: You have a history of failing to follow through on things you initiate. Why should this undertaking be any different?
- Speed killer: If you can't lose weight fast, kill the diet.

If any of the above apply to you in beginning Phase Two, replace them, using your affirmation or discipline tactics. Remember that negative feelings take time and practice to overcome. I designed Phase Two to last longer than Phase One because it takes longer to change attitudes than to change eating habits.

I learned how to overcome my feelings of boredom—and even to put joy and enthusiasm back into my diet—by watching and talking to thin people. I found that while they do watch their calorie intake, they do so not with strict regimentation but with flexible control. When thin people get bored with a particular food, they simply switch to another in the same family—like going from chicken to turkey or fish, from animal-protein foods to vegetable-protein foods, or from pasta dishes to bean-and-rice combinations. The important thing was that *whatever changes they made, they did not markedly increase their calorie intake.* This, I realized, was the key to my continued weight loss. With a little more flexibility than I had allowed myself during Phase One, I could still control my 800-calorie daily intake but have much greater freedom in food selection.

If you want to add flexibility to your diet *without adding extra calories,* simply decide which foods you want to try, then look up these items in your calorie counter. If their calories according to recommended portion sizes are not comparable, you can make them so by eating smaller portions. However, this does *not* mean it's all right for you to revert to eating cookies, cakes, or fried foods. Regardless of portion sizes, such rich, high-calorie foods have very little nutritive value; in addition, these items can easily become binge triggers.

Also, try new lean preparation techniques. Instead of slicing, chop; rather than sectioning, slice. And if you've been broiling or boiling, try steaming or poaching. Experiment with new no-calorie or low-calorie taste seasonings, too.

Expand your repertoire of eating places beyond your kitchen or dining-room table. Have breakfast on your front porch, or lunch in the park instead of at your desk or in the company cafeteria. If you feel confident with your ability to discipline your Fat Self and maintain your total daily calorie limit, try a new restaurant.

Above all, continue to affirm your thinning perspective and to acknowledge your accomplishments. Take pleasure in buying new clothes to fit your changing figure, and remind yourself often of how much better you feel, both physically and emotionally.

Big Diet Plateaus

Three months into Phase Two, I hit my first big diet plateau: the numbers on my bathroom scale did not move for several weeks. I was concerned. I knew from experience that plateaus of such duration could spell doom for my diet. Instead of allowing my Fat Self to dictate a dump-the-diet response, I called my doctor. He explained to me that plateaus are the body's resting and readjustment periods. The body has been working extremely hard "eating itself up" and becoming more efficient at metabolizing energy from stored body fat. Metabolism and kidneys, the body's fluid regulators, are continually readjusting once weight loss begins. When a big plateau occurs, the metabolism has simply become more economic in burning calories. As the kidneys adjust to the decrease in sodium being metabolized, less water is eliminated from the body. The plateau ends when the kidneys and metabolism have completed the readjustment. To hasten this metabolic process, my doctor recommended that I cut my daily calories from 800 to 700 for two weeks. I followed his advice, and over the next five and a half weeks I lost 22 pounds.

Big diet plateaus never bothered me again.

If you experience a big diet plateau, check with your doctor before cutting calories below 800 per day. Even if he or she gives you the go-ahead, bear in mind that going below 800 calories, even for just a week or two, is very hard work.

If you are feeling even slightly deprived, or if you have been having difficulty sticking to the 800-calorie plan, do not attempt to reduce your level any further. Instead, use your time strategy again to shore up your thinning perspective. Remind yourself, daily if necessary, that you know what's going on inside your body and therefore do not need your Fat Self's advice, which is to quit dieting. (During a big diet plateau, your Fat Self will tell you that calorie reduction does not result in weight loss, only in feelings of deprivation. You, however, know better.)

Putting Insatiable Hunger in Perspective

Insatiable hunger has a fearsome reputation among overweighters, and for good reason. It has prevented many from even trying to lose weight. For others, it has discredited them and their diet efforts, turning both into failures. No one, it is said, can withstand the power of real hunger pangs for very long. However, the truth is that real hunger pangs do pass, and fairly quickly.

Insatiable hunger—the kind that cannot be satisfied no matter how much food you eat—has little to do with the body's physical need for food. In her book *The Obsession: Reflections on the Tyranny of Slenderness*, Kim Chernin talks about hunger ultimately being "a yearning for permission to enjoy the sensual aspects of the self." For most overweighters, food is the primary means used to satisfy this yearning, or appetite, for life's sensual pleasures. When I felt insatiable hunger, I was aware that I was hungry for more than food. I wanted to feel loved and accepted by myself and others and to feel safe and well cared for. I knew that I used food to fulfill these normal

119

human yearnings. Unfortunately, however, this awareness did not stop the insatiable hunger my Fat Self thrust upon me.

To put these yearnings in perspective, I recommend that you do as I did—get involved in pleasurable activities that divert your attention away from your growling stomach and your Fat Self's incessant demands for food to fill what is really an emotional hunger. Taking a walk, visiting a friend, reading a good book or attending a concert or a movie—even cleaning your house—can help.

The important thing is to understand and acknowledge that, *over time*, these alternate activities will replace eating as the primary means for fulfilling your emotional yearnings.

Although you may find it hard to believe, this *will* happen. In Phase One, you learned to replace fat foods and habits with thin ones, and as a result you lost weight. The replacement process you engage in now is just the same; only this time, you are replacing your fat activities with thin ones. It is just one more part of replacing your diet mentality.

The Physical Changes from Fat Body to Thin Body

Marcia Millman, in *Such a Pretty Face: Being Fat in America*, spotlights the overweighter's extreme difficulty in accepting the physical changes that accompany weight loss. The transition from looking overweight to looking slender, she observes, is loaded with fantastical expectations of becoming a god- or goddesslike body lithely moving through a problem-free world. This idea, of course, is sponsored by the Fat Self, which is now desperate to recapture lost pounds.

Another problem in making the transition from fat to thin lies in self-image. During Phase Two, as I lost the last two-thirds of my excess weight, the change in my appearance was dramatic. However, internally all was the same: my self-image was still that of a fat person. Of course, this was my Fat Self's doing—another of its techniques to get me to regain the weight I'd lost.

It quickly became apparent to me that I would not be able to maintain an external thin look without a corresponding internal feeling of thinness. Once again, I turned to my Thin Self for guidance in helping me to grow.

The closer you get to reaching your ideal weight, the more questions you will have about the changes you see in your body. For example, you may wonder if your thin body will seem like a stranger to you; whether you will get skin wrinkles; whether your muscles will look flabby and jiggle the way your fat did; and what you should do about clothes. The answers to these questions will come, as they did for me, as you continue to lose weight.

The physical changes you experience present opportunities not only for growing thin, but for growing emotionally and mentally. You have a choice to make about how you will respond now to the physical changes that occur in your body. Let your thinning perspective help you make that choice, not your Fat Self. Realistically, the physical changes, troublesome though your Fat Self may try to make them, are joyful changes.

Let's look at the major kinds of change you can expect to experience as a result of weight loss: increased physical energy; lag time between actually getting thin and seeing yourself as thin; and the transition from "such a pretty face" to the real thing.

Increased Physical Energy

You do not have to engage in an exercise regimen to enjoy the increased physical energy and muscle strength of your lighter body. Not only will you move more easily and freely, you will want to move more frequently. Acting on this desire is how you begin to tighten and tone your muscles. The long muscles (i.e., back and leg) can be tightened even more by continuous, sustained movement.

The degree to which you can tighten your loose skin depends on several factors: your age, the length of time you were overweight, how much weight you lost, the degree and frequency of your previous diets, and your gender. For example, a 25-year-old woman losing 30 pounds for the first time has more elasticity to her skin than I did. I suggest that you consult your doctor—he or she may recommend specific exercises to help you tighten your skin.

How you respond to your body's desire for more physical movement during Phase Two is up to you. Instead of taking the elevator at work or in your apartment building, you might choose to walk up the stairs. Rather than taking public transportation or driving your car everywhere, walking may be just the ticket for short distances. The point is that your thinning body will seek outlets for its increased physical energy. Help it find them by using your thinning perspective and your common sense.

Lag Time: From Looking Thin to Feeling Thin

Many dieters find that their external appearance changes long before their self-image changes. Their bodies look thin, but they still *feel* like fat people.

An example of this lag time might include looking at your new, smaller clothes and thinking you can't really fit into them. Another example—one that happened to me a lot—is glancing at your reflection in a plate-glass window and not recognizing yourself.

Lag time ceases when your self-image merges with your external appearance. Be prepared for your Fat Self to fight this merging by trying to convince you that your lean look is temporary and therefore you should continue to wear your old, fat clothes. I recommend strongly that you buy new clothes and discard old ones each time you go down a few sizes; continuing to wear your fat clothes—or even just keeping them in your closet—is like inviting your Fat Self to stick around.

Following are several body-awareness exercises you can do to help your self-image catch up with your external appearance.

Standing before your full-length mirror, stretch, bend,

and twist your body from side to side, keeping your hands on the muscles you're moving so that you can feel what your eyes refuse to see. Continue this exercise throughout Phase Two. As your body continues slimming down, you will feel a growing suppleness.

On the stairs or walking down the street, place your hands on your hips and feel them swivel as your legs move. Listen for the sound of your footfalls. As your weight decreases, the sound will change.

After bathing, skin lotions, fresheners, or moisturizing creams can be used as "touch tools" for increasing your body awareness.

What your Fat Self refuses to acknowledge with your eyes, your hands confirm. As your weight decreases, so do the layers of fat around your body. Your hands will notice the absence of these layers before your eyes do. In these exercises, feeling is believing. And believing that your body is thin is what having a thin self-image is all about.

The Transition from "Such a Pretty Face" to the Real Thing

After lag time concludes, there is one more kind of change ahead of you: genuine acceptance of your slenderness. As you take your body inventory at the conclusion of Phase Two, you will be at your ideal weight. While appraising the assets and imperfections of your thin body, be careful not to fall into the trap of unrealistic expectations.

When making my own physical appraisal, I wanted to be stunningly beautiful. I don't believe there's a dieter alive who doesn't want to be both thin and physically striking. But what do you do if you're not a Candice Bergen or a Farrah Fawcett (or, for you men, a Robert Redford or Burt Reynolds)? What do you do when the thin person in the mirror is merely yourself?

Once again, you listen to the voice of your Thin Self, which will tell you honestly and realistically how you look. You may hear words like "wonderful," "courageous," "outstanding," or "simply stunning." These are apropos of both your personal accomplishment and your physical appearance.

You will have body imperfections, just as every other thin person does. Genuine acceptance means learning to love your thin body, imperfections and all, simply because it's yours.

CHAPTER NINE

Phase Three: Maintaining Weight Loss

THE GOAL OF PHASE THREE is to replace your Fat Self's emotional domination over you and your food. In effect, you will replace your Fat Self with your Thin Self.

You accomplish this by increasing your calories up to maintenance levels without increasing your weight; dealing with your emotional feelings without feeding them; and finally, completing the transition from fat feelings–thin body to thin feelings–thin body.

Stopping the Weight-Loss Process

You end the weight-loss process by increasing your calorie intake to a maintenance level for your ideal weight. To determine what your level is, multiply your ideal weight by 12 if you are female, 15 if you are male. For example, if you are medium-framed, female, five feet seven inches, your ideal weight is about 140 pounds. If you multiply this weight times

12, you find your maintenance calorie level is in the high 1600 range. *(This level does not take into account a moderate daily exercise regimen.)*

It is not wise to increase your calories all at once; to do so could be too great a shock to your metabolism, and you might even start gaining back your weight. I suggest you follow my doctor's recommendation to me: each week, add 200 to 300 calories to your daily level, until you reach your maintenance level. (For example, during the first week of Phase Three, bring your daily level up to 1000 calories; during the second week, increase to 1200, and so on.)

Do *not* make your increases in any one single food group or at random. Be guided by your nutrition goals as you plan your menus for the first several weeks of Phase Three.

The following chart shows you how to add calories to the various food groups while maintaining good nutritional balance.

Comparative Menu Chart: 800–2300 Calories

		800	1000	1200	1500	1800	2100	2300
Group 1:	Meat and Meat Alternatives	200	200	200	250	250	350	400
Group 2:	Milk and Milk Products	100	100	100	100	200	250	300
Group 3:	Vegetables	150	200	300	375	450	550	600
Group 4:	Fruits	150	200	200	200	200	250	300
Group 5:	Whole Grains and Cereals	150	200	300	375	450	450	450
Group 6:	Visible Fats	0	50	50	150	200	200	200
Group 7:	Snacks	50	50	50	50	50	50	50

You will notice that between 800 and 1200 calories, the recommended increases occur in 200-calorie increments; moving from 1200 to 1800, there are two 300-calorie increases, and three 300-calorie increases between 1200 and 2300 calories. If you feel comfortable making increases at these recommended levels, do so *one week at a time.* Feel free, however, to make your increases more slowly (for instance, every two weeks rather than once a week). Let your Thin Self be your guide in determining what's best for you.

If You Gain Weight (And You Didn't Overeat)

Scientists are currently studying lipoproteins, which influence the body's conversion of calories into energy, to learn why some individuals metabolize proteins and fats more efficiently than complex carbohydrates, and why other individuals fare better in weight maintenance with vegetables, grains, and cereals than with meats.

When you are overweight, your metabolism is fat-geared. You gained weight because you ate too much animal protein, or too much carbohydrate, or too much fat.

After reaching your ideal weight, some of you may discover that you gain weight relatively easily eating recommended proportions of whatever nutrient you overate in the past. In my case, I found that the recommended 300 calories for whole grains and cereals was too high for me—I gained weight from it. It was not that I was overeating; it was just that my body did not metabolize complex carbohydrates as well as it metabolized other nutrients. So, I cut 100 calories from the whole-grains-and-cereals group, and added 100 calories to the recommended number for meats, which my body metabolized quite efficiently.

If you find that you gain weight easily eating the recommended number of calories for any one food group, simply cut some of those calories, then add the same number to a food group that your body metabolizes more efficiently. Or, add back the number of calories by dividing it over several groups. For example, if you gain weight easily eating meats and decide to cut 200 calories from the recommended number, try adding back 50 calories in fruits, 100 calories in milk and milk products, and 50 in whole grains and cereals. The numbers on your bathroom scale will guide you in making these adjustments.

Your bathroom scale will also tell you about the sodium

content of the foods you've added to your diet in Phase Three. As you know, sodium helps your body retain water. As you increase your calories, you will also be increasing your sodium consumption. Be patient. Your kidneys and your metabolism need time to adjust, just as they did during the two weight-loss phases. In time, you will pass off the excess water and your weight will return to normal. If you want to hasten the return, simply cut back a little on the foods that are high in sodium, or switch to foods marked "low salt" or "no salt added."

Learning to Eat Exactly Like Other Thin People

Thin people maintain their weight not only by varying their food selections without increasing calories, but by balancing high-calorie days with low-calorie days. They do not "diet"; yet, when the need arises, they do cut back on calories.

In my prediet days, I had enviously watched thin people in line at the ice-cream parlor, eating rich desserts at restaurants, ordering popcorn with butter at the movies—seeming, in fact, to eat whatever they wanted whenever they wanted it, without gaining weight. Now, as I began Phase Three, I learned their secret: they did eat whatever they wanted, but *not* whenever they wanted to. In observing and listening to my thin friends, I discovered that they did, almost without exception, cut back on calories the day after a cookie binge or a hot fudge sundae. After a big holiday meal, they generally cut back on calories for several days. Always, they maintained a balance.

I remember clearly the first time I allowed myself a special treat. A friend had baked brownies; they were still warm from the oven, and they looked and smelled delicious. I *wanted* one. But what if I used it as a binge trigger? What if that first bite of brownie ended up as the first step in regaining all the weight I'd lost? As these fears ran through my mind, I realized that it was only my Fat Self trying to keep me in the old diet mentality—trying to keep me thinking like a fat person. In truth, there was nothing to fear. I knew that a brownie has approximately 200 calories; I also knew that I could eat that brownie and make up for it the following day, by staying 200 calories below my maintenance level. The feeling of freedom that came with this realization is something I will never forget.

Now that you have reached your ideal weight, you, too, will begin to eat just as normally thin people do. But you have an advantage here: your food awareness is much better developed than theirs. As you prepare now for the occasional high-calorie days that are sure to come, you will use that food awareness to maintain your weight.

How to Stop Feeding Your Feelings

Eating can be a very pleasurable activity. Not all people eat for the pleasure of it, though. Thin and overweight people alike often eat to alleviate unpleasant feelings. The essential difference between a thin person and a fat person going through the cookie jar alone on a Saturday night because of loneliness or boredom or sexual frustration—or any other unpleasant feeling—is that the thin person cuts back on calories over the next day or two in order to prevent weight gain, while the overweighter does not.

About halfway through Phase Three, I experienced a period of extreme loneliness. Of course, I'd had that feeling before; prediet, I'd eaten my way through such times; during Phase One and Phase Two, I'd learned to focus my attention on other activities so that I did not give in to my desire to overeat. Now, however, the old feeling was back—I wanted to binge to avoid feeling lonely. Yet, I knew that binging wouldn't really help; the loneliness would still be there afterward. Substitute activities weren't the answer either now, because at best they were only temporary. And I wanted a permanent solution.

I realized that in order to deal constructively with my loneliness—or any other negative feeling—I would have to face the feeling directly. I would have to acknowledge it and allow myself to experience it. I knew it would be painful, but the pain couldn't be more than that of regaining my weight.

129

The following steps are those that helped me learn to deal with my feelings directly.

Step 1: Give yourself permission to have the feeling.

Step 2: Separate the feeling from the situation that is causing it.

Step 3: Use one or several of the following means to release the feeling:

- breathe deeply
- express emotion in crying, yelling, laughing
- redirect the feeling by hitting a pillow or pounding a wall
- engage in vigorous physical action like singing, running, dancing, or aerobics

Step 4: Once the feeling is experienced and released, take whatever action is necessary to respond to the situation that caused the feeling (for example, confront the co-worker whose criticisms of you are causing you stress on the job).

Step 5: Use one or several of the following stress-management techniques:

- meditation
- regular physical exercise
- sensible balance between work and play
- relaxation exercises
- frequent reminders that you need not be perfect

Your Emotions

You may find that now, as a thin person, you feel more emotional, more vulnerable. You no longer have your fortress of fat to "protect" you. Perhaps you feel so emotionally deprived that you just can't cope, or you feel sorry for yourself, or you feel you are the victim of your circumstances. Perhaps living thin isn't what you thought it would be, so you get angry. Whatever the feeling, be prepared for your Fat Self to try to rescue or comfort you with food. (You can also be overwhelmed by feelings of exuberance and joy, with the same result—your Fat Self will encourage you to celebrate it in an expansive way, by expanding your mouth and your waistline.)

Whatever emotions you feel now, you will feel them differently—and perhaps more intensely—than you used to. Expect other people to react to that difference (often negatively). As a result of following your personal food-plan diet, you are stronger and more direct. This is good for you, but upsetting to those in your immediate circle of family, friends, and co-workers. For example, as an overweight person you probably had to appease others (and yourself) in order to be accepted. Now you don't need to. In fact, you are likely to be quite angry about having "had" to do that. You are also likely to be somewhat self-centered and demanding. This is a normal and necessary *phase* in learning to live thin emotionally. You are simply experiencing the emotions you've had all along; the difference is that prediet, these emotions were damped out by overeating.

Depending on the degree and period of time you have expressed an emotionally dependent relationship with food, in thinning from the inside out, you will become more consciously aware of choice in developing relationships with yourself and others that are less personally destructive and more personally growth promoting.

Relating to Others

In relating to others as an overweight person, you are a stereotype, and others respond to you as such. When you relate now as a thin person, you are an individual among individuals. You learn now that you can take care of yourself, get attention, receive and give affection, feel safe, be liked, be "in charge" or in control of situations, and be generous enough to give to others.

People who knew you when you were fat have to adjust now to your dramatic change. Be patient with them. It may take time for them to stop walking on eggshells when they are with you and begin to treat you like an ordinary person. You are one of them now, but they may, at first, resist your giving up your role as sympathetic listener, victim, or ugly duckling.

Some people may pressure you to return to your former way of eating. Perhaps your relationship with them was based on eating together, or being fat together, and they miss this. If such people continue to give you mixed messages about your weight, (telling you that you look great, while encouraging you to overeat with them), see less of them, or develop new relationships.

One of the most exciting things you will experience now is meeting new people—people who never knew you as fat. This provides a wonderful opportunity to explore yourself, to get to know who the thin you really is, and to get to know others without your old fat barrier in the way. Most important, new friends, by their acceptance of you as a thin person, help to strengthen your new image of yourself.

Maintaining Weight Loss

There is no question that losing weight is difficult. Permanently maintaining that loss will also be difficult. You may even think it more difficult, because you must continue to "watch your weight" for as long as you want to remain thin. You must actively work at it.

As you conclude Phase Three, you are living thin. You will encounter problems, but they need not bring back the problem of living fat.

You have learned the principles of permanent weight

management. Now you must choose either to continue applying them or to abandon them. It is the same choice you made at the start of this program: do you want to live fat, or do you want to live thin?

PART THREE

Living Thin and the Role of Exercise

CHAPTER TEN

The Need for Exercise in Your Thin Life

IN MOST PEOPLE'S MINDS, DIET and exercise are closely associated; they believe you can't successfully do one without doing the other. But that's simply not true. I lost 120 pounds without exercising. However, I could not maintain my ideal weight now without regular, vigorous exercise.

It was not until I was thin that I began to understand how essential exercise is to maintaining normal weight, muscle tone, efficient metabolic functions, and emotional well-being.

Dieters tend to think of exercise almost exclusively in terms of its physical benefits: helping you to get in shape and burn calories quickly. Thin people, on the other hand, think of exercise as a way of life—not as a means to an end. Now that you are no longer overweight, you should think of exercise not just in terms of your weight but in terms of its contribution to your overall physical and emotional well-being.

There are, however, certain misconceptions about exercise; being aware of them will help you overcome your fears and resistance in this area.

Misconceptions About Exercise

• *You have to exercise in order to lose weight.*

The truth is, you don't have to. Your body moves around anyway during your normal daily activities, and as your weight lessens, your physical movements will increase. You may have to nudge your body out of your favorite chair once in a while; you do not have to take aerobics classes.

• *If you exercise, you get to eat more.*

That may be true for professional athletes, but for you, this thought, especially in the hands of your Fat Self, can destroy your diet.

After Phase Two, you *can* eat cake and ice cream and other goodies, but only when you feed them to your Thin Self once in a while as treats, not as rewards to your Fat Self for working up a little sweat.

• *You must exercise all the time and for the rest of your life if you expect to stay thin.*

The truth is, you should exercise when you need to—and you, not your Fat Self, are the best judge of that need. Your Fat Self would like you to think you have to exercise all the time, just as it had you believe that you would have to "be on a diet" for the rest of your life. The purpose of this misconception is to instill fear in you so that you do nothing about your weight problem.

• *You have to like exercising in order to do it.*

You may not enjoy exercise in the beginning, because your Fat Self will put up a lot of resistance. You must overcome this resistance just as you overcame resistance to dieting. If you do not replace this resistance, you will give your Fat Self a strong power base from which to make a comeback.

Under the influence of your Fat Self, exercise can become actual physical punishment. Your Fat Self may urge you to overexercise—with the result that you exhaust or injure yourself. Beware of this. Your Fat Self can't stand the idea of a healthy body, and exercise will give you the healthy body you want.

• *Exercise can replace the compulsion to overeat.*

Exercise is an alternative activity to overeating: it cannot replace a compulsive desire to overeat. Compulsive eaters find that when their exercise schedules are interrupted—due to pressures of time, the cancellation of a friend's participation, a body injury, or inclement weather—their compulsive eating habits return. Instead of spending their time in the gym, they return to the kitchen.

Benefits of Exercise

In addition to tightening your body muscles and improving your metabolic functions, exercising is a terrific way to make new friends and enrich your social life. It can also relieve the pressures, disappointments, and anxieties we all experience from time to time. When you exercise, you feel more in control of your life, and this leads to a sense of well-being.

A quick swim at a local pool, a brisk walk, even pedaling your exercycle while watching TV can help to relieve tensions. That release can be even more beneficial to you than burning up calories.

Exercise for Living Thin

You have a choice in your exercise regimen. Rather than jumping into a swimming pool when you don't know how to swim, or signing up for a gym twenty miles away in the dead of winter, use your common sense in choosing exercises that are convenient and familiar to you. You might want to practice a variety of exercises, based on weather conditions, your emotional needs, your income level, and the availability of exercise partners.

When you do choose to exercise, either during your program or soon after you conclude it, advise your doctor; he or she will alert you to any dangers to your physical health. In addition, check with your local YMCA or other organizations that can help you plan a fitness program suited to your lifestyle, needs, and preferences.

Like me, you will find not only that you feel better about yourself when you exercise, but that exercise is essential to living thin.

Appendix:
My Personal Menus

800-Calorie Food Plan: Phase One Menus

VARIETY IS THE MAINSTAY OF reduced-calorie food plans. Without a daily variety of foods from each of the principal groups, you run the risk of either dumping the diet because of boredom, or endangering your health because you're not getting adequate nutrition.

My seven Phase One menus reflect what for me were the most important foods. I selected adequate portions of meat, milk, fruits, vegetables, grains, and cereals, and used herbs, spices, and low- or no-calorie sauces (see pp. 184–185) to enhance taste. Although these menus are nutritionally balanced, my doctor recommended that I take a daily multiple vitamin-mineral tablet, and I suggest you do the same.

Bear in mind that the following menus reflect *my* preferences. Yours may be quite different. Feel free to follow my menus if they appeal to you. If they do not, simply use them as guidelines for drawing up your own.

	DAY 1	
		Calories
BREAKFAST	1 hard-boiled egg	80
	½ orange, quartered	30
		110
LUNCH	Open-Faced Tuna Sandwich	
	½ 6½-ounce can water-packed	
	tuna, drained, flaked	110
	1 teaspoon spicy mustard	8
	1 slice whole-wheat bread	60
	½ tomato, sliced	15
	¼ onion, sliced	10
	2 iceberg lettuce leaves	4
		207
AFTERNOON SNACK	½ orange, quartered	30
DINNER	Herbed Chicken	
	Sprinkle:	
	½ chicken breast, skinned	155
	With:	
	herbs and spices to taste	0
	Broil in preheated broiler 15 minutes	
	Serve with:	
	1 cup fresh carrots, sliced, steamed	50
	1 small (2½-inch diameter) white	
	potato, steamed	90
		295
EVENING SNACK	Salad	
	Combine in bowl:	
	¼ head iceberg lettuce, shredded	15
	½ tomato, wedges	15
	¼ onion, sliced	10
	½ medium carrot, sliced	10
	¼ cup fresh green beans, chopped	8
	¼ medium cucumber, sliced	8
	1 tablespoon lemon juice	4
	herbs and spices to taste	0
		70
	1 cup nonfat milk for coffee and tea	90
	total calories	802

DAY 2

BREAKFAST Open-Faced Apple Sandwich

1 slice whole-wheat bread	60
1 tablespoon nonfat yoghurt	8
½ medium apple, sliced	40
1 teaspoon raisins	12
dash of cinnamon	0
	120

LUNCH Tuna Salad
Combine in bowl:

½ 6½-ounce can water-packed tuna, drained, flaked	110
½ tomato, chopped	15
¼ cup celery, chopped	5
¼ onion, chopped	10
½ medium apple, chopped	40
¼ head iceberg lettuce, shredded	15
½ cup carrots, chopped	25
1 teaspoon raisins	12
	232

DINNER Liver in Wine Sauce
Simmer in 8-inch skillet 8–10 minutes:

¼ cup red wine	0
¼ cup water	0
¼ onion, chopped	10
½ cup mushrooms, sliced	10
1 garlic clove, pressed	3
herbs and spices to taste	0

Add and simmer 5 minutes:

4 ounces beef liver, sliced	156

Serve with:

½ cup frozen spinach, cooked	28
1 small (2½-inch diameter) white potato, steamed	90
	297

EVENING SNACK Salad (see Evening Snack—Day 1) 70

1 cup nonfat milk for coffee and tea 90

total calories 809

DAY 3

BREAKFAST	1 hard-boiled egg	80
	1 slice whole-wheat bread	60
	½ medium apple, spears	40
		180

LUNCH — Fruit and Yoghurt Plate
Arrange on plate:

¼ cup nonfat yoghurt	31
½ medium apple, spears	40
¼ pear, spears	25
¼ cup strawberries, halved	14
⅓ medium banana, small spears	33

Top with:

1 teaspoon raisins	12
dash of cinnamon	0
	155

DINNER — Lemon Chicken
Sprinkle:

½ chicken breast, skinned	155

With:

1 tablespoon lemon juice	4
herbs and spices to taste	0

Broil 15 minutes in preheated broiler
Serve with:

½ cup fresh broccoli, steamed	20
½ cup fresh cauliflower, steamed	14
½ cup fresh green beans, steamed	16
1 small (2½-inch diameter) white potato, steamed	90
	299

EVENING SNACK	2 cups air-popped popcorn	50
	½ orange, quartered	30
		80

1 cup nonfat milk for coffee and tea	90

total calories 804

DAY 4

BREAKFAST | 1 slice whole-wheat bread | 60
| ½ ounce cheddar cheese | 53
| ¼ medium apple, spears | 20
| | 133

LUNCH | Fruit and Raw Vegetable Plate |
| ¼ medium apple, spears | 20
| ⅓ medium banana, small spears | 33
| ¼ pear, spears | 25
| ½ cup carrot spears | 25
| ½ cup zucchini spears | 9
| ¼ cup cauliflower | 7
| 1 teaspoon raisins | 12
| ½ ounce cheddar cheese | 53
| | 184

AFTERNOON SNACK | ⅓ medium banana | 33
| ½ cup strawberries, halved | 28
| 1 cup nonfat milk | 90
| | 151

DINNER | Baked Fish |
| Place in ovenproof dish: |
| ½ onion, sliced | 20
| 4 ounces red snapper | 105
| 1 tablespoon lemon juice | 4
| herbs and spices to taste | 0
| Bake at 350° 15–20 minutes |
| Serve with: |
| ½ cup frozen spinach, cooked | 28
| 1 small (2½-inch diameter) white |
| potato, steamed | 90
| | 247

1 cup nonfat milk for coffee and tea | 90

total calories 805

DAY 5

BREAKFAST   Fruit and Yoghurt Plate (see Lunch,
Day 3)   155

LUNCH   1 slice whole-wheat bread   60
1 hard-boiled egg   <u>80</u>
140

DINNER   Steak and Vegetables
Broil in preheated broiler 10–15
minutes:
   4 ounces lean round steak   214
   herbs and spices to taste   0
Serve with:
   $\frac{1}{2}$ cup carrots, steamed   25
   $\frac{1}{2}$ cup green beans, steamed   16
   1 small ($2\frac{1}{2}$-inch diameter) white
   potato, steamed   <u>90</u>
345

EVENING
SNACK   Salad (see Evening Snack, Day 1)   70

1 cup nonfat milk for coffee and tea   90

total calories 800

DAY 6

		Calories
BREAKFAST	Open-Faced Apple Sandwich (see Breakfast, Day 2)	120
LUNCH	Fruit and Raw Vegetable Plate (see Lunch, Day 4)	184
DINNER	Broil in preheated broiler 10–15 minutes:	
	4 ounces lean ground beef	248
	herbs and spices to taste	0
	Serve with:	
	½ cup frozen spinach, cooked	28
	1 small (2½-inch diameter) white potato, steamed	90
		366
EVENING SNACK	1 cup air-popped popcorn	25
	1 cup nonfat milk for coffee and tea	90
	total calories	785

147

DAY 7

		Calories
BREAKFAST	1 hard-boiled egg	80
	½ orange, quartered	30
		110

LUNCH — Open-Faced Tuna Melt Sandwich
Assemble in order and broil until hot:

	Calories
1 slice whole-wheat bread	60
1 teaspoon spicy mustard	8
½ 6½-ounce can water-packed tuna, drained, flaked	110
1 tablespoon grated cheddar cheese	20

Serve with:

	Calories
½ medium apple, sliced	40
	238

AFTERNOON SNACK — ½ orange, quartered — 30

DINNER — Chicken in Wine Sauce
Simmer in 8-inch skillet 8–10 minutes:

	Calories
¼ cup white wine	0
¼ cup water	0
¼ onion, chopped	10
½ cup sliced mushrooms	10
1 garlic clove, pressed	3
herbs and spices to taste	0

Add and simmer, covered, 15 minutes:

	Calories
½ chicken breast, skinned	155

Serve with:

	Calories
½ cup green beans, steamed	16
½ cup sliced beets, steamed	33
1 small (2½-inch diameter) white potato, steamed	90
	326

	Calories
1 cup nonfat milk for coffee and tea	90

total calories 785

800-Calorie Food Plan: Phase Two Menus

The following Phase Two 800-calorie menus offer a greater variety of foods from the principal groups, without increasing total calories.

New foods I included were three kinds of fish, chicken liver, cottage cheese, grapefruit, oatmeal, rice, flour tortillas, and plain bagels.

Again, you may follow my menus, or you may draw up your own to meet your needs and preferences.

DAY 1

		Calories
BREAKFAST	Oatmeal Special	
	Prepare according to package directions:	
	¼ cup rolled oats	110
	Top with:	
	¼ pear, sliced	25
	¼ medium apple, sliced	20
	1 teaspoon raisins	12
	1 packet sugar substitute	4
	¼ cup nonfat milk	23
	dash of cinnamon	0
		194
LUNCH	Cucumber Crunch	
	Combine in bowl:	
	1 cup cubed cucumber	20
	1 tomato, diced	30
	½ onion, diced	20
	½ green bell pepper, diced	7
	¼ cup nonfat yoghurt	31
	1 tablespoon lemon juice	4
	pinch of dill and ground pepper	0
		112
AFTERNOON SNACK	Fruit Plate	
	¼ pear, spears	25
	¼ medium apple, spears	20
	¼ medium banana, small spears	25
		70
DINNER	Broiled Steak and Peppers	
	Place in ovenproof dish:	
	4 ounces lean round steak	214
	½ onion, sliced	20
	½ green bell pepper, sliced	7
	2 tablespoons red wine	0
	herbs and spices to taste	0

Broil in preheated broiler 10–15 minutes
Serve with:
½ cup cooked white rice	90
½ cup zucchini, steamed	9
	340
1 cup nonfat milk for coffee and tea	90

total calories 806

DAY 2

BREAKFAST One-Egg Omelet
Sauté in small nonstick skillet
5 minutes:

¼ onion, diced	10
¼ tomato, diced	8

Add and heat:

¼ cup steamed cauliflower	7
¼ cup steamed zucchini	5
herbs and spices to taste	0

Cook over low heat in 8-inch nonstick
skillet until set

1 egg, beaten	80

Add heated vegetables to egg and
fold in half
Top with:

1 tablespoon grated cheddar cheese	20

Serve with:

¼ orange, sliced	15
	145

LUNCH Open-Faced Apple Sandwich

1 slice whole-wheat bread	60
1 tablespoon nonfat yoghurt	8
½ medium apple, sliced	40
1 teaspoon raisins	12
dash of cinnamon	0
	120

AFTERNOON SNACK

½ medium banana, sliced	50
½ cup nonfat milk	45
	95

DINNER Broiled Lemon Cod
Place in ovenproof dish:

½ onion, sliced	20
4 ounces cod	88
2 tablespoons white wine	0
herbs and spices to taste	0
½ lemon, sliced	10

Broil in preheated broiler
10–15 minutes
Serve with:

½ cup cooked white rice	90
½ cup sliced carrots, steamed	25
8 asparagus spears, steamed	24
	257

EVENING	1 pink grapefruit, halved, broiled	92
SNACK	dash of cinnamon	0
	1 cup nonfat milk for coffee and tea	90

total calories 799

DAY 3

BREAKFAST | Yoghurt and Fresh Fruit
Combine in bowl:

1/4 cup nonfat yoghurt	31
1/2 medium apple, chunks	40
1/4 pear, chunks	25
1/3 medium banana, sliced	33
1/4 cup grapes	28
dash of cinnamon	0
	157

LUNCH | Open-Faced Tomato Sandwich
Assemble in order:

1 slice whole-wheat bread	60
1 teaspoon spicy mustard	8
1/2 tomato, sliced thin	15
1/4 green bell pepper, sliced thin	4
1/2 ounce cheddar cheese, sliced thin	53
dash of chili powder and paprika	0

Broil in preheated broiler until hot and cheese melts
Serve with:

1/4 orange, sliced thin	15
	155

DINNER | Sashimi at Home
Arrange on plate:

4 ounces albacore, raw, sliced thin	200
1 tablespoon soy sauce, mixed with:	10
1 tablespoon horseradish	11

Garnish with:

1 carrot, curled strips	20
1/2 cup cooked white rice	90
	331

EVENING SNACK | Salad
Combine in bowl:

1/4 head iceberg lettuce, shredded	15
1/2 tomato, wedges	15
1/4 onion, sliced	10
1/2 carrot, sliced	10
1/4 cup fresh green beans, chopped	8
1/4 medium cucumber, sliced	8
1 tablespoon lemon juice	4
herbs and spices to taste	0
	70
1 cup nonfat milk for coffee and tea	90

total calories 803

DAY 4

BREAKFAST Oatmeal Special (see Breakfast, Day 1) 194

LUNCH Sliced Egg on Lettuce
Assemble:
  1 hard-boiled egg, sliced 80
  2 iceberg lettuce leaves 4
  1 carrot, sticks 20
  ½ cup raw green beans, sliced 16
  ½ cup raw zucchini, sliced 9
  dash of paprika and ground pepper 0
  129

AFTERNOON Fruit Plate (see Afternoon Snack, Day 1) 70
SNACK

DINNER Broiled Lemon Chicken
Place in ovenproof dish
  ½ chicken breast, skinned 155
  2 tablespoons white wine 0
  2 garlic cloves, minced 6
  herbs and spices to taste 0
  ½ lemon, sliced thin 10
Broil in preheated broiler 15–20 minutes
Serve with:
  ½ cup cooked white rice 90
  ½ cup broccoli, steamed 20
  ½ cup cauliflower, steamed 14
  295

EVENING ¼ medium apple, sliced 20
SNACK

  1 cup nonfat milk for coffee and tea 90

total calories 798

DAY 5

BREAKFAST Puffed Cheese Tortilla
Heat in nonstick skillet:

1 9-inch flour tortilla	169
Top with:	
1 tablespoon grated cheddar cheese	20
Serve with:	
¼ orange, sliced thin	15
	204

LUNCH Fruit and Raw Vegetable Plate

¼ medium apple, spears	20
⅓ medium banana, small spears	33
¼ pear, spears	25
¼ cup grapes	28
½ cup zucchini spears	9
½ cup broccoli	20
¼ cup cauliflower	7
1 carrot, spears	20
	162

DINNER Wine-Simmered Chicken Livers
Simmer in 8-inch skillet 8–10 minutes:

¼ cup white wine	0
¼ cup water	0
¼ onion, chopped	10
½ cup sliced mushrooms	10
1 garlic clove, pressed	3
herbs and spices to taste	0
Add and simmer 5 minutes:	
4 ounces chicken livers, sliced	187
Serve with:	
½ cup cooked white rice	90
½ cup sliced beets, steamed	33
½ cup fresh green beans, steamed	16
	349

1 cup nonfat milk for coffee and tea	90
total calories	805

DAY 6

BREAKFAST Spinach Omelet
Sauté in small nonstick skillet:

	Calories
¼ onion, diced	10
¼ tomato, diced	8
1 cup fresh raw spinach, chopped	14

Cook on low heat in 8-inch nonstick
skillet until set:

1 egg, beaten	80

Add heated vegetables to egg and
fold in half
Top with:

1 tablespoon grated cheddar cheese	20
	132

LUNCH Cottage Cheese with Bagel

½ plain bagel	81
¼ cup low-fat cottage cheese	50
1 teaspoon raisins	12
dash of cinnamon	0

Serve with:

½ orange, quartered	30
½ medium apple, sliced	40
	213

AFTERNOON Fruit Plate (see Afternoon Snack,
SNACK Day 1)   70

DINNER Poached Sole
Simmer in 8-inch skillet:

¼ cup white wine	0
¼ onion, chopped	10
¼ cup chopped celery	5
1 garlic clove, pressed	3
½ lemon, sliced thin	10

Add and simmer 5 minutes:

4 ounces sole	90

Serve with:

½ cup cooked white rice	90
½ cup sliced carrots, steamed	25
½ cup broccoli, steamed	20
½ cup cauliflower, steamed	14
	267

EVENING SNACK	½ pink grapefruit, broiled	46
	dash of cinnamon	0
		46
	1 cup nonfat milk for coffee and tea	90
	total calories	818

DAY 7

BREAKFAST	Yoghurt and Fresh Fruit (see Breakfast, Day 3)	157
LUNCH	Sliced Egg on Lettuce (see Lunch, Day 4)	129
AFTERNOON SNACK	½ apple, sliced	40

DINNER   Chicken in Red Mushroom Sauce
Simmer in 8-inch skillet 5 minutes:

¼ cup red wine	0
¼ cup water	0
1 cup sliced mushrooms	20
½ onion, sliced	20
2 garlic cloves, pressed	6
herbs and spices to taste	0

Add and simmer, covered, 15 minutes:

½ chicken breast, skinned	155

Serve with:

½ cup cooked white rice	90
1 cup broccoli, steamed	40
	331

EVENING SNACK

2 cups air-popped popcorn	50
dash of dill	0
	50

1 cup nonfat milk for coffee and tea	90

total calories 797

Phase Three Menus: 1000 Calories, 1200 Calories

The following 1000- and 1200-calorie Phase Three menus reflect an even greater variety. I designed these meals with the knowledge that I would eat them for the rest of my thin life.

DAY 1, 1000 CALORIES

		Calories
BREAKFAST	Yoghurt and Fresh Fruit	
	Combine in bowl:	
	¼ cup nonfat yoghurt	31
	½ medium apple, chunks	40
	¼ pear, chunks	25
	⅓ medium banana	33
	¼ cup grapes	28
	dash of cinnamon	0
		157
LUNCH	Tofu Burrito	
	Heat in small nonstick skillet:	
	½ onion, chopped	20
	¼ cup canned kidney beans, drained and rinsed	55
	¼ cup cooked white rice	45
	Gently fold in:	
	2 ounces firm tofu, drained, chopped	41
	½ ounce grated cheddar cheese	53
	Roll up filling in:	
	1 9-inch flour tortilla, warmed	169
		383
DINNER	Roasted Orange Chicken	
	Place in ovenproof dish:	
	1 teaspoon oil	41
	½ onion, sliced	20
	½ chicken breast, skinned	155
	1 tablespoon orange juice	5
	2 tablespoons white wine	0
	½ orange, sliced thin	30
	Surround chicken with:	
	1 carrot, julienned	20
	1 celery stalk, julienned	7
	Roast uncovered at 375° for 30–35 minutes	

Serve with:
½ cup Brussels sprouts, steamed	25
½ cup sliced beets, steamed	33
¼ cup cooked white rice	45
	381
½ cup low-fat milk for coffee and tea	70
total calories	991

DAY 2, 1000 CALORIES

Calories

BREAKFAST Puffed Cheese Tortilla and Fruit
Heat in nonstick skillet:
    1 9-inch flour tortilla   169
Top with:
    1 tablespoon grated cheddar
    cheese   20
Serve with:
    1/2 mango, sliced   44
    1/2 cup strawberries   <u>28</u>
    261

LUNCH Sweet Tuna Salad
Combine in bowl:
    1/2 6 1/2-ounce can water-packed
    tuna, drained, flaked   110
    1/4 cup chopped celery   5
    1/4 onion, chopped   10
    1/2 medium apple, chopped   40
    1 teaspoon raisins   12
    1/4 cup nonfat yoghurt   31
    1 tablespoon low calorie
    mayonnaise   40
    1/2 ounce bulgur wheat, dry   <u>50</u>
    298

Chill for 30–40 minutes

AFTERNOON Raw Vegetable Plate
SNACK   1 carrot, spears   20
    1/2 cup zucchini spears   9
    1/2 cup fresh green beans   16
    1/4 cucumber, sliced   8
    1/2 tomato, wedges   <u>15</u>
    68

DINNER Pasta and Vegetable Casserole
Blend and place in ovenproof dish:
    1/2 cup cooked macaroni   78
    1/2 cup broccoli, steamed   20
    1/2 cup cauliflower, steamed   14
    1/4 cup fresh peas, steamed   29
    1/2 cup zucchini, steamed   9
Top with:
    1 ounce grated cheddar cheese   <u>105</u>
    255

Bake at 350° 20–30 minutes

EVENING SNACK ½ medium apple, sliced 40

½ cup low-fat milk for coffee and tea 70

total calories 992

DAY 3, 1000 CALORIES

BREAKFAST	Oatmeal Special	
	Prepare according to package directions:	
	¼ cup rolled oats	110
	Top with:	
	¼ pear, chunks	25
	½ medium apple, chunks	40
	1 teaspoon raisins	12
	1 packet sugar substitute	4
	¼ cup nonfat milk	23
		214
LUNCH	Open-Faced Egg Sandwich	
	Assemble in order:	
	½ English muffin	70
	1 tablespoon low-calorie mayonnaise	40
	½ onion, sliced thin	20
	½ tomato, sliced thin	15
	1 hard-boiled egg, sliced	80
	herbs and spices to taste	0
	Serve with:	
	½ medium apple, wedges	40
		265
DINNER	Baked Salmon	
	Place in ovenproof dish:	
	¼ onion, sliced	10
	4 ounces salmon steak	246
	¼ cup white wine	0
	herbs and spices to taste	0
	½ lemon, sliced	10
	Bake at 350° 20–30 minutes	
	Serve with:	
	½ cup sliced carrots, steamed	25
	½ cup fresh peas, steamed	58
	½ cup cooked white rice	90
		439
EVENING SNACK	½ cup papaya cubes	36
	½ cup low-fat milk for coffee and tea	70
	total calories	1024

DAY 4, 1000 CALORIES

Calories

BREAKFAST Curried Tofu Omelet	
Sauté in small nonstick skillet:	
1 teaspoon oil	41
¼ onion, diced	10
½ tomato, diced	15
1 garlic clove, minced	3
¼ cup cooked white rice	45
¼ teaspoon each paprika, curry powder, cinnamon	0
Gently fold in:	
2 ounces firm tofu, drained, chopped	41
Cook over low heat in 8–10-inch nonstick skillet until set:	
2 egg whites, beaten with:	34
2 teaspoons water	0
Add heated vegetables to egg and fold in half	
Serve with:	
½ orange, quartered	30
½ small whole-wheat pita bread, heated	63
Topped with:	
¼ cup nonfat yoghurt	31
1 teaspoon raisins	12
	325
LUNCH Vegetable Soup	
Heat in medium saucepan 10–15 minutes:	
1½ cups water	0
½ cup red wine	0
2 vegetable bouillon cubes	12
¼ cup sliced carrots	12
½ cup broccoli pieces	20
½ cup fresh green beans, sliced	16
¼ cup corn	35
¼ cup cooked white rice	45
¼ cup cooked macaroni	39
herbs and spices to taste	0
	179
AFTERNOON SNACK Fruit Plate	
½ medium apple, spears	40
½ pear, spears	50
¼ mango, sliced	22
½ medium banana, small spears	50
	162

```
DINNER    Steamed Shrimp and Potato
          Steam and arrange on plate:
              4 ounces raw shrimp, peeled,
              deveined                              103
              1 small (2½-inch diameter)
              white potato                           90
          Mix for sauce:
              ¼ cup nonfat yoghurt                   31
              1 tablespoon lemon juice                4
              1 teaspoon dill                         0
              1 teaspoon spicy mustard                8
          Serve with:
              ½ cup sliced beets, steamed            33
                                                    ─────
                                                     269

              ½ cup low-fat milk for coffee and tea  70

                                  total calories 1005
```

DAY 5, 1000 CALORIES

BREAKFAST Cold cereal and Fruit

1 ounce bite-size shredded wheat	110
½ cup nonfat milk	45
¼ medium apple, chunks	20
¼ pear, chunks	25
½ cup strawberries, sliced	28
1 tablespoon raisins	36
1 packet sugar substitute	4
	268

LUNCH Sandwich and Salad
Mix in bowl and chill 30 minutes:

¼ head iceberg lettuce	15
1 tomato, wedges	30
½ cup chopped celery	10
2 scallions, chopped	8
½ ounce bulgur wheat, dry	50
2 tablespoons lemon juice	8
herbs and spices to taste	0

Serve with:

½ bagel	81

Topped with:

1 tablespoon nonfat yoghurt	8
1 teaspoon raisins	12
	222

AFTERNOON SNACK

½ cup strawberries	28

DINNER Liver and Onions
Sauté in nonstick skillet 5 minutes:

½ tablespoon oil	62
½ onion, sliced	20

Add and sauté on medium-high heat 5–10 minutes:

4 ounces beef liver	156
herbs and spices to taste	0

Serve with:

½ cup sliced carrots, steamed	25
½ cup fresh green beans, steamed	16
1 small (2½-inch diameter) white potato, steamed	90
	369

EVENING SNACK	½ pink grapefruit, broiled	46
	½ cup low-fat milk for coffee and tea	70
	total calories	1003

DAY 6, 1000 CALORIES

		Calories
BREAKFAST	Oatmeal Special (see Breakfast, Day 3)	214
LUNCH	Spinach Omelet	
	Sauté in small nonstick skillet:	
	1 teaspoon oil	41
	¼ onion, diced	10
	½ cup sliced mushrooms	10
	1 garlic clove, minced	3
	1 cup fresh raw spinach,	
	chopped	14
	2 tablespoons cooked white rice	23
	¼ ounce bulgur wheat, dry	25
	Remove from heat and fold in:	
	1 tablespoon nonfat yoghurt	8
	1 tablespoon grated cheddar	
	cheese	20
	Cook on low heat in 8–10-inch nonstick	
	skillet until set:	
	2 eggwhites, beaten with:	34
	2 teaspoons water	0
	Add heated vegetables to egg and	
	fold in half	
	Serve with:	
	½ plain bagel	81
	Topped with:	
	1 tablespoon nonfat yoghurt	8
	1 teaspoon raisins	12
		289
AFTERNOON SNACK	½ orange, sliced	30
DINNER	Meat and Potato	
	Broil in preheated broiler	
	10–15 minutes	
	4 ounces lean round steak	214
	herbs and spices to taste	0
	Serve with:	
	1 small (2½-inch diameter) white	
	potato, baked	90
	Topped with:	
	1 tablespoon nonfat yoghurt	8
	dash of dill and ground pepper	0

And: 1 cup mixed vegetables, steamed:
$\frac{1}{3}$ cup sliced carrots   17
$\frac{1}{3}$ cup peas   39
$\frac{1}{3}$ cup beets   <u>22</u>
         390

$\frac{1}{2}$ cup low-fat milk for coffee and tea   70

total calories 993

DAY 7, 1000 CALORIES

Calories

BREAKFAST Puffed Cheese Tortilla and Fruit (see
Breakfast, Day 2)   261

LUNCH English Tuna Sandwich
Mix in bowl:
    1/2 6½-ounce can water-packed
    tuna, drained 110
    2 tablespoons nonfat yoghurt 16
    1 teaspoon raisins 12
Serve on:
    1/2 English muffin 70
    208

DINNER Chicken and Tofu Stir-Fry
Stir-fry in 8–10-inch nonstick skillet
5 minutes:
    1/2 cup sliced broccoli 20
    1/4 cup sliced cauliflower 7
    1/2 cup sliced green beans 16
    1/4 cup peas 29
    1/2 cup sliced carrots 25
Add and stir-fry 5–10 minutes:
    4 ounces boneless chicken,
    skinned, sliced 155
    1 tablespoon soy sauce 10
    2 tablespoons water 0
Fold in gently:
    2 ounces firm tofu, drained, cubed 41
Serve with:
    1/2 cup cooked white rice 90
    393

EVENING SNACK 1 cup papaya cubes 72

1/2 cup low-fat milk for coffee and tea 70

total calories 1004

170

DAY 1, 1200 CALORIES

BREAKFAST Scrambled Egg
Sauté in small nonstick skillet 5 minutes:

¼ onion, chopped	10
Add and stir gently:	
2 egg whites, beaten with:	34
2 teaspoons water	0
And: 2 ounces firm tofu, drained, chopped	41
Serve with:	
½ orange, sliced	30
1 slice whole-wheat bread	60
1 tablespoon nonfat yoghurt	8
1 teaspoon raisins	12
	195

LUNCH Tabbouli and Pita
Mix and chill 30 minutes:

1 ounce bulgur wheat, dry	100
½ tomato, diced	15
2 scallions, chopped	8
2 tablespoons chopped parsley	4
½ tablespoon oil	62
herbs and spices to taste	0
Serve with:	
1 small whole-wheat pita	125
	314

AFTERNOON SNACK Fruit Plate

½ medium apple, spears	40
½ pear, spears	50
½ cup strawberries	28
	118

DINNER Red Sauce and Steak over Noodles
Simmer in 8–10-inch nonstick skillet
10 minutes:

¼ cup red wine	0
½ onion, chopped	20
1 cup sliced mushrooms	20
1 tomato, chopped	30
herbs and spices to taste	0
Remove from heat, cool slightly, and add:	
¼ cup nonfat yoghurt	31
Pour over:	
½ cup cooked egg noodles	100
4 ounces lean round steak, broiled	214

Serve with:
    ½ cup fresh peas, steamed   58
    ½ cup sliced carrots, steamed   25
                                498

½ cup low-fat milk for coffee and tea   70

total calories 1195

DAY 2, 1200 CALORIES

BREAKFAST Cereal and Fruit

1 ounce bite-size shredded wheat	110
½ cup nonfat milk	45
¼ medium apple, chunks	20
¼ pear, chunks	25
½ cup sliced strawberries	28
1 teaspoon raisins	12
1 packet sugar substitute	4
	244

LUNCH Soup and Salad

Simmer in medium saucepan
30 minutes:

1 beef bouillon cube	6
1 cup water	0
½ cup cooked lentils	107
2 tablespoons barley, dry	86
½ cup sliced carrots	25
½ cup chopped celery	10
½ onion, chopped	20
1 clove garlic, pressed	3
herbs and spices to taste	0

Serve with:

¼ head iceberg lettuce, shredded	15
1 tomato, wedges	30
½ cucumber, sliced	15
1 tablespoon lemon juice	4
dash of dill and ground pepper	0
	321

AFTERNOON SNACK

1 cup papaya cubes	72
¼ cup nonfat yoghurt	31
	103

DINNER Broiled Salmon

Place in ovenproof dish:

½ onion, sliced thin	20
¼ cup white wine	0
4 ounces salmon	246
dash of dill	0
½ lemon, sliced thin	10

Broil in preheated broiler
10–15 minutes
Remove, cool slightly, and
add to sauce:

¼ cup nonfat yoghurt	31

Serve with:

½ cup cooked white rice	90
½ cup broccoli, steamed	20
½ cup cauliflower, steamed	14
½ cup sliced carrots steamed	25
	456
½ cup low-fat milk for coffee and tea	70
total calories	1194

DAY 3, 1200 CALORIES

BREAKFAST Puffed Cheese Tortilla and Fruit
Heat in nonstick skillet:

1 9-inch flour tortilla	169

Top with:

1 tablespoon grated cheddar cheese	20

Serve with fruit bowl:

½ mango, sliced	44
⅓ medium banana, chunks	33
¼ cup sliced strawberries	14
½ cup grapes	56
¼ cup nonfat yoghurt	31
dash of cinnamon	0
	367

LUNCH Omelet
Sauté in small nonstick skillet:

½ onion, diced	20
½ tomato, diced	15
¼ cup cooked white rice	45
½ cup canned garbanzo beans, drained	105

Cook over low heat in 8–10-inch
nonstick skillet until set:

2 egg whites, beaten with:	34
2 teaspoons water	0

Add heated vegetables to eggs and
fold in half
Sprinkle with:

½ ounce grated cheddar cheese	53

Serve with:

2 kiwi, peeled, sliced	20
½ orange, sliced	30
	322

AFTERNOON Raw Vegetable Plate
SNACK

½ cup broccoli spears	20
½ cup cauliflower florets	14
½ cup zucchini spears	9
	43

DINNER Chicken and Mushroom Casserole
Place in order listed in ovenproof dish:

½ cup red wine	0
1 tablespoon barley, dry	43
½ tablespoon oil	62
1 tablespoon lemon juice	4
1 clove garlic, minced	3

```
              ¼ onion, diced                         10
              1 cup sliced mushrooms                 20
              ½ chicken breast, skinned             155
              herbs and spices to taste              0
      Bake at 375° 30 minutes
      Remove, cool slightly, and add to sauce:
              ¼ cup nonfat yoghurt                   31
      Serve with:
              ½ cup sliced carrots, steamed          25
              ¼ cup cooked white rice                45
                                                    ‾‾‾
                                                    398

      ½ cup low-fat milk for coffee and tea         70

                              total calories 1200
```

BREAKFAST Spanish Omelet
Sauté in small nonstick skillet
5–10 minutes:

1 teaspoon oil	41
1/4 onion, diced	10
1/2 tomato, diced	15
1/4 cup cooked white rice	45
1/4 cup canned kidney beans, drained, rinsed	55

Remove, cool slightly, and add:

1/4 cup nonfat yoghurt	31
1/4 teaspoon each chili powder, paprika, black pepper	0

Cook over low heat in 8–10-inch
nonstick skillet until set:

2 egg whites, beaten with:	34
2 teaspoons water	0

Add heated vegetables and fold in half
Sprinkle with:

1/2 ounce grated cheddar cheese	53

Serve with:

1/2 mango, sliced	44
	328

LUNCH Chicken and Potato Soup
Simmer in medium saucepan 20 minutes:

2 chicken bouillon cubes	12
1/2 cup white wine	0
1 tablespoon lemon juice	4
1 tablespoon barley, dry	43
1 small (2 1/2-inch diameter) white potato, diced	90
1/4 cup cooked white rice	45
1/2 cup diced carrots	25
1/2 onion, diced	20
1/4 cup fresh peas	29
4 ounces steamed chicken, diced	155
herbs and spices to taste	0
	423

DINNER Pasta and Vegetable Casserole
Blend and place in ovenproof dish:

1/2 cup cooked macaroni	78
1 carrot, sliced, steamed	20
1/2 cup broccoli, steamed	20
1/2 cup cauliflower, steamed	14
1/2 cup sliced zucchini, steamed	9
1/4 cup fresh peas, steamed	29
1/4 cup nonfat yoghurt	31

Top with:
    1 ounce grated cheddar cheese   <u>105</u>

                                       306

Bake at 350° until heated, 15–20 minutes

EVENING SNACK   1 cup papaya cubes   72

     ½ cup low-fat milk for coffee and tea   70

total calories 1199

DAY 5, 1200 CALORIES

BREAKFAST Scrambled Egg and Bagel
Mix and sauté over low heat in
nonstick skillet:

2 egg whites	34
1 teaspoon water	0
1 tablespoon nonfat yoghurt	8
1 tablespoon grated cheddar cheese	20

Serve with:

1/2 plain bagel	81
	143

LUNCH Tofu Burrito
Heat in small nonstick skillet:

1/2 onion, diced	20
1/4 cup canned kidney beans, drained, rinsed	55
1/4 cup cooked white rice	45

Gently fold in:

2 ounces firm tofu, drained, chopped	41
1/2 ounce grated cheddar cheese	53

Roll up filling in:

1 9-inch flour tortilla, heated	169
	383

AFTERNOON SNACK Fruit Salad
Mix in bowl:

1/4 cup nonfat yoghurt	31
1/2 medium apple, chopped	40
1/4 pear, chopped	25
1/2 cup halved strawberries	28
dash cinnamon	0
	124

DINNER Roasted Orange Chicken
Place in ovenproof dish:

1 teaspoon oil	41
1/2 onion, sliced	20
1/2 chicken breast, skinned	155
1 tablespoon orange juice	5
1/4 cup white wine	0
herbs and spices to taste	0
1/2 orange, sliced thin	30

Surround chicken with:

1 carrot, julienned	20
1 celery stalk, julienned	7

Roast uncovered at 375° 30–35 minutes

Serve with:

	½ cup Brussels sprouts, steamed	25
	½ cup sliced beets, steamed	33
	¼ cup cooked white rice	<u>45</u>
		381
EVENING	1 cup papaya cubes	72
SNACK	1 cup air-popped popcorn	<u>25</u>
		97
	½ cup low-fat milk for coffee and tea	70

total calories 1198

DAY 6, 1200 CALORIES

BREAKFAST Cereal and Fruit (see Breakfast, Day 2)   244

LUNCH Tofu Burrito and Fruit
Heat in small nonstick skillet:

½ onion, chopped	20
¼ cup canned kidney beans, drained, rinsed	55
¼ cup cooked white rice	45

Gently fold in:

2 ounces firm tofu, drained, chopped	41
½ ounce grated cheddar cheese	53
1 tablespoon nonfat yoghurt	8

Roll up filling in:

1 9-inch flour tortilla, heated	169

Serve with:

½ medium banana, sliced	50
	441

DINNER Shrimp Stir-Fry
Stir-fry in 8–10-inch nonstick skillet
5 minutes:

½ tablespoon oil	62
½ cup sliced broccoli	20
¼ cup sliced cauliflower	7
½ cup sliced mushrooms	10
¼ cup sliced carrots	12
¼ cup fresh peas	29
¼ cup corn	35

Add and stir-fry 5 minutes:

4 ounces raw shrimp, peeled, deveined	103
1 tablespoon lemon juice	4

Serve with:

½ cup cooked white rice	90
	372

EVENING

½ mango, sliced	44
¼ cup nonfat yoghurt	31
	75

SNACK

½ cup low-fat milk for coffee and tea	70

total calories 1202

DAY 7, 1200 CALORIES

BREAKFAST Oatmeal Special
Prepare according to package
directions:

¼ cup rolled oats	110

Top with:

¼ pear, chunks	25
½ medium apple, chunks	40
½ cup sliced strawberries	28
1 teaspoon raisins	12
1 packet sugar substitute	4
½ cup nonfat milk	45
dash of cinnamon	0
	264

LUNCH Pasta Salad
Combine in bowl and chill:

½ cup cooked macaroni	78
½ cup nonfat yoghurt	62
½ cup sliced broccoli, steamed	20
½ cup sliced carrots, steamed	25
½ cup fresh peas, steamed	58
¼ cup Brussels sprouts, steamed	12
1 ounce cheddar cheese, shredded	105
	360

DINNER Liver and Onions
Sauté in nonstick skillet
5 minutes:

½ tablespoon oil	62
½ onion, sliced	20

Add and sauté on medium-high heat
5–10 minutes:

4 ounces beef liver	156
herbs and spices to taste	0

Serve with:

½ cup green beans, steamed	16
½ cup sliced carrots, steamed	25
½ cup sliced beets, steamed	33
1 small (2½-inch diameter) white potato, steamed	90

Topped with:

1 tablespoon nonfat yoghurt	8
dash of dill, ground pepper	0
	410

EVENING SNACK	½ pink grapefruit, broiled	46
	2 cups air-popped popcorn	50
		96
	½ cup low-fat milk for coffee and tea	70
	total calories	1200

LOW- AND NO-CALORIE SAUCES

Calories

FOR MEAT, POULTRY AND FISH

1 tablespoon horseradish	11
1 tablespoon nonfat yoghurt	8
	19

1 teaspoon spicy mustard	8
1 tablespoon nonfat yoghurt	8
	16

Simmer:

½ cup water	0
2 tablespoons lemon juice	8
¼ onion, chopped	10
¼ green pepper, chopped	4
1 garlic clove, chopped	3
¼ tomato, chopped	8
pinches of parsley, basil, thyme, salt substitute, ground pepper	0
	33

FOR RAW OR COOKED VEGETABLES

¼ cup nonfat yoghurt	31
dill or curry to taste	0
	31

¼ cup nonfat yoghurt	31
1 tablespoon grated cheddar cheese	20
pinches of paprika, salt substitute, ground pepper	0
	51

Simmer:

2 ounces canned clams and juice	30
¼ onion, chopped	10
1 garlic clove, chopped	3
¼ cup chopped celery	5
1 teaspoon lemon juice	1
2 tablespoons white wine	0
Cool and add:	
¼ cup nonfat yoghurt	31
1 tablespoon chopped parsley	2
	82

BREAD SPREADS

1 tablespoon nonfat yoghurt	8
¼ apple, sliced	20
1 teaspoon raisins	12
	40

1 teaspoon spicy mustard	8
1/4 tomato, sliced	8
1/4 onion, sliced	10
1 tablespoon grated cheddar cheese	20
	46

SALAD DRESSINGS

2 tablespoons lemon juice	8
1 tablespoon water	0
pinches of dill, ground pepper, salt substitute	0
	8

1/4 cup nonfat yoghurt	31
2 teaspoons spicy mustard	16
1/2 packet sugar substitute	2
	49

1/4 cup nonfat yoghurt	31
2 teaspoons rice vinegar	0
1/2 packet sugar substitute	2
pinches of basil, thyme, ground pepper, salt substitute	0
	33

Afterword

In the words of Abraham, 'Go thou and do likewise,' even if not
identically. Be your own personal success.

Nancy L. Wilson, R.D.

ELIZABETH LAY'S BOOK TRACES HER passage from morbidly
fat (240 pounds) to normally thin (120 pounds). The result is
one long dreamed of by dieters—transformation from fat person, through formerly fat person, to one who eats normally and
without constant preoccupation with food. Elizabeth's system
is unique: it teaches overweighters how to "live thin" for the
rest of their lives.

I had taken Elizabeth's personal accomplishment for
granted until I began to study the success rates of most dieters.
I was shocked to discover that only a small number reached
their weight goal, and that fewer still were able to maintain
their weight loss for long. In the mental-health field in general,
two-thirds of all patients recover with some form of help. Even
the addictive disorders such as drug and alcohol abuse have a
fairly high recovery rate. Yet, obesity persists and eating disorders abound. Estimates are that 95 percent of all dieters will
regain their lost weight within five years. Many will end up
heavier than before. In light of that, Elizabeth's accomplishment is all the more remarkable.

The gradual reshaping of food desires, attitudes, and

habits is crucial to enable the overweight person to carry through his or her decision to lose weight permanently. Far-reaching changes of this type must begin with honesty and clear decision. These changes can be maintained only if the person builds a net of habits and awarenesses that can support the new direction he or she has taken. Elizabeth's thinning perspective, in which maintenance, rather than weight loss per se, is the real issue, accomplishes this very effectively. Her success clearly shows that overweight people *can* break the pattern of cyclical dieting and constant preoccupation with food.

Many of Elizabeth's diet tactics for losing weight resemble behavior-modification techniques. However, her approach differs from that of the behavior-modification programs in one subtle but important area: the locus of control. Compulsive overeaters experience the self as being controlled by their desires, which are viewed as being outside the self. Behavior-modification capitalizes on this to promote weight loss by having dieters alter their surroundings and change the reinforcement pattern to one that supports eating reduced quantities of food or less-fattening types of food. Elizabeth's system, on the other hand, supports dieters in taking responsibility for themselves, so that they can locate, and change, the point of control inside themselves.

The Fat Self and Thin Self constructs that dieters learn to use are drawn from Gestalt psychotherapy. But, as with the behavioral-change techniques, they are applied in a unique manner. Instead of their being a dialog between the two subpersonalities, they are instead devices used by the dieter to develop and maintain appropriate self-control.

As a result, *Thinning from the Inside Out* provides the harried and frustrated dieter with a new and valid hope. Elizabeth shows you how to replace the diet mentality with a thinning perspective, and carry that through into true weight maintenance. Her book, and her personal experience, can inspire as well as guide this process.

Mary Tall, Ph.D
Clinical Psychologist
November 1985

188

Recommended Reading

Self-Watching and Self-Help

Fat Is a Feminist Issue: A Self-Help Guide for Compulsive Eaters, by Susie Orbach. Berkley Books.

The Obsession: Reflections on the Tyranny of Slenderness, by Kim Chernin. Harper Colophon Books.

The Road Less Traveled: A New Psychology of Love, Traditional Values and Spiritual Growth, by M. Scott Peck, M.D. Simon and Schuster Touchstone Book.

Self-Watching, Addictions, Habits, Compulsions: What to Do About Them, by Ray Hodgson and Peter Miller. Facts on File Publications.

Such a Pretty Face: Being Fat in America, by Marcia Millman. Berkley Books.

Personal Success Stories

The James Coco Diet, by James Coco. Bantam Books.

Mary Ellen's Help Yourself Diet Plan, by Mary Ellen Pinkham. St. Martin's Press/Marek.

Nutrition Books and Calorie Counters

The Brand-Name Nutrition Counter, by Jean Carper. Bantam Books.

Food & Drink Counter. Dell Purse Book, Dell Publishing Co.

Jane Brody's Nutrition Book, by Jane E. Brody. Bantam Books.

What's In What You Eat, by Will Eisner. Bantam Books.

Index

191

ABOUT THE AUTHOR

Elizabeth Lay lives and works in the San Francisco Bay Area where she maintains her literary agency. She has post-graduate degrees in literature and education. She writes magazine articles and occasional book reviews. She is currently working on her second book.